Hodder Gibson

Scottish Examination Mate

INTERMEDIATE 2 /HIGHER

ENGLISH

Developing Skills in Textual Analysis

Dr Susan MacDonald

Hodder Gibson

A MEMBER OF THE HODDER HEADLINE GROUP

INTRODUCTION

Exercises in textual analysis are challenging — particularly in poetry. You are trying to comment on the ideas of poems which you have probably never seen before and without the help of a teacher.

This book is meant to guide you through the stages of analysis and to give you some confidence in expressing your opinion on the poems. Each poem is accompanied by a set of notes. An annotated copy of the poem is included at the back of the book. These notes and annotations may give you some ideas, but you should try to become increasingly independent in answering the questions on each of the poems. You may disagree with the ideas expressed here about the poems. The questions are in the style of the Intermediate and Higher examinations with marks assigned to each question. The less you rely on the notes and ideas of others in answering the questions, the more you are expressing your own opinion. You may think sometimes that you could show your understanding of the poem better without so many questions. However, the questions make it easier for markers to assess your understanding of the poem — and they are also meant to focus on key parts of the poem.

Some of the poems may seem easier to understand than others, but that can be a matter of opinion too. You should also remember that your opinions can not be 'wrong' as long as you can give reasons for thinking as you do, supported by references to the text of the poem. The last poem offers some comments on the questions and sample answers which you might like to look at after you have tried the questions on your own.

Think of each poem as a puzzle. You are trying to see the overall picture — the ideas the poet is trying to express. You also want to comment on how well you think the ideas are expressed. Do you like the poem? What do you like about it? Do you agree with the ideas? Express your ideas fully and confidently.

Although every effort has been made to ensure that website addresses are correct at time of going to press, Hodder Gibson cannot be held responsible for the content of any website mentioned in this book. It is sometimes possible to find a relocated web page by typing in the address of the home page for a website in the URL window of your browser.

Papers used in this book are natural, renewable and recyclable products. They are made from wood grown in sustainable forests. The logging and manufacturing processes conform to the environmental regulations of the country of origin.

Orders: please contact Bookpoint Ltd, 130 Milton Park, Abingdon, Oxon OX14 4SB. Telephone: (44) 01235 827720. Fax: (44) 01235 400454. Lines are open from 9.00 – 5.00, Monday to Saturday, with a 24-hour message answering service. Visit our website at www.hoddereducation.co.uk. Hodder Gibson can be contacted direct on: Tel: 0141 848 1609; Fax: 0141 889 6315; email: hoddergibson@hodder.co.uk

© Susan MacDonald 2002
First published in 2002 by Robert Gibson and Sons Ltd.
This edition published by
Hodder Gibson, a member of the Hodder Headline Group
2a Christie Street
Paisley PA1 1NB

Impression number   10 9 8 7 6 5 4 3 2
Year   2010 2009 2008 2007 2006

Printed and bound in Great Britain by Martins the Printers, Berwick-upon-Tweed

A catalogue record for this title is available from the British Library

ISBN-10: 0-716-96019-2
ISBN-13: 978-0-716-96019-5

TABLE OF CONTENTS

DESCRIPTIVE POEMS

The first two poems in this collection are descriptions of places. They are unusual descriptions because each poem is viewing the landscape from above — from a height or a god-like perspective.

First consider the poem *Football at Slack* by Ted Hughes. Try to annotate or comment on a copy of the poem. Then compare your copy with the one on page 58.

♦ Read the poem through and accept that probably it will not make much sense at first reading. Poetry is highly condensed. The reader has to work at understanding.

FOOTBALL AT SLACK

Between plunging valleys, on a bareback of hill
Men in blunting colours
Bounced, and their blown ball bounced.

The blown ball jumped, and the merry-coloured men
5   Spouted like water to head it.
The ball blew away downwind —

The rubbery men bounced after it.
The ball jumped up and out and hung on the wind
Over a gulf of treetops.
10   Then they all shouted together, and the ball blew back.

Winds from fiery holes in heaven
Piled the hills darkening around them
To awe them. The glare light
Mixed its mad oils and threw glooms.
15   Then the rain lowered a steel press.

Hair plastered, they all just trod water
To puddle glitter. And their shouts bobbed up
Coming fine and thin, washed and happy

While the humped world sank foundering
20   And the valleys blued unthinkable
Under the depth of Atlantic depression —

But the wingers leapt, they bicycled in air
And the goalie flew horizontal

And once again a golden holocaust
25   Lifted the cloud's edge, to watch them.

Ted Hughes

♦ Do you see anything unusual in the poem's form? It is written in stanzas, but they are irregular. Some have three lines, some four and one five. The last two have only two each. This irregular pattern is unusual in poetry and it may be important in appreciating the ideas. Note also that it does not seem to rhyme.

♦ Next try to decide what the poet is writing about in the first three lines.

> Between plunging valleys, on a bareback of hill
> Men in blunting colours
> Bounced, and their blown ball bounced.

This seems to be a football game which is taking place between two men's teams in a small village at Slack, somewhere in the hills.

In the first line the words 'plunging' and 'bareback' stand out as being unusual. Do you see any connection between them? They might both be connected to horses. 'Plunging' suggests the way a horse moves, almost rolling up and down. 'Bareback' suggests the smooth rounded back of the horse with a slight dip in the centre. Or you might imagine a small boat plunging between big waves. It is easy to see how the poet is using these words metaphorically — to describe the ups and downs of hills and valleys and the smooth tops of rounded hills.

The other feature of the first stanza which you might notice is the number of 'b's': 'blunting', 'Bounced', and 'blown ball bounced'. Here, you have to use your imagination. Alliteration is used usually to draw attention to something important. It might be drawing attention to the idea of the constantly moving ball.

♦ In the second stanza you might notice unusual combinations of subjects and verbs.

> The blown **ball jumped**, and the merry-coloured **men**
> 5 **Spouted** like water to head it.
> The ball blew away downwind —

The first one is 'ball jumped'; this is personification which suggests that the ball has a life of its own. The second one is the 'men / Spouted like water'. You have to ask yourself: in what way could a group of men be likened to water? They would look like water if they were all moving or *flowing* in the same direction — *like a steady stream*. This is what would be happening in a fast-moving game where the men were following the movement of the ball up and down the field and from side to side. Therefore, you could say that this is an effective image because it helps you picture better the events of the game.

5

♦ In stanza three, the poet continues to use this technique of personification.

> The rubbery men bounced after it.
> The ball jumped up and out and hung on the wind
> Over a gulf of treetops.
> 10 Then they all shouted together, and the ball blew back.

The ball is likened to a person in 'jumped' and he makes the men sound like the ball in 'rubbery', further suggesting that their movement is like bouncing. Also notice the alliteration which ends the stanza and draws your attention to the ball again: 'the **b**all **b**lew **b**ack'. These first three stanzas are effective in describing the football game, the movements of both the men and the ball.

♦ Then in the next stanza the poet draws our attention to the sky.

> Winds from fiery holes in heaven
> Piled the hills darkening around them
> To awe them. The glare light
> Mixed its mad oils and threw glooms.
> 15 Then the rain lowered a steel press.

It seems as if the winds are coming from 'fiery holes in heaven'. You have to use your imagination. What could be fiery holes in the sky? Breaks in the clouds where the red sun is shining through?

And the winds are personified. He makes them sound like a great god who is piling clouds on the distant hills.

Two more images in the stanza make the picture more vivid. 'Mad oils' suggests that the landscape is like an oil painting — although perhaps 'mad' doesn't make much sense to you.

The final image is possibly the most effective as the rain starts to fall heavily — 'lowered a steel press'. You can imagine all the sharp prongs of a press like the sheets of constant, heavy rain. This stanza is very effective in describing the landscape through these four vivid images.

♦ The fifth stanza gives an impression of how wet the scene becomes after the rain.

> Hair plastered, they all just trod water
> To puddle glitter. And their shouts bobbed up
> Coming fine and thin, washed and happy

You should note in your jottings words like 'hair plastered' and 'trod water'. The phrase 'puddle glitter' particularly suggests the light on the water. With 'shouts bobbed up', the poet could almost be suggesting that the men are bobbing up and down in the water.

♦ The next stanza continues this impression.

> While the humped world sank foundering
> 15 And the valleys blued unthinkable
> Under the depth of Atlantic depression —

The word 'humped' reminds us of the setting of rounded hills and 'blued' suggests again the sky with holes in the clouds.

♦ The final two stanzas, unusually short, are a final confirmation of the action — action which continues no matter what the weather.

> But the wingers leapt, they bicycled in air
> And the goalie flew horizontal
>
> And once again a golden holocaust
> 20 Lifted the cloud's edge, to watch them.

The verbs 'leapt', 'bicycled' and 'flew' suggests that the game is as active as ever. 'Bicycled' is particularly appropriate in suggesting the movement of the men's legs as they leap into the air and 'horizontal' is a good description of a goalie saving a ball, flying crosswise in the effort.

In the final two lines the poet leaves the field and takes a look at the sky again as the sun reappears in a 'golden holocaust'. He suggests with the word 'lifted' that the sun is like a person lifting the edge of a blanket in order to watch the men's game below.

After you have taken all these notes, ask yourself if any ideas or any techniques particularly stand out. The poem is about movement: it makes the men sound like balls and the balls sound like men — an unusual perspective. It also suggests a lot about the surroundings — the colour and the light of the sky, the shape of the hills and the valleys, and especially the rain. It seems to be taking a sort of artist's perspective of a game of football. It is not counting the goals or appreciating the individual actions of the men, but describing the beauty of the entire scene and experience. Word choice, imagery and alliteration have been used particularly to create this scene.

If you take such notes on your copy of the poem, you should be able to answer the questions which are intended to guide you into expressing your appreciation of such ideas and the use of such techniques. The value given to the question could indicate how many reasons or explanations you need to give in the answer; the value could also be indicating the difficulty of the question. You should try to answer each question as fully as possible, giving your own ideas and perhaps original, individual interpretation. If you can justify your point of view by supporting your remarks with reference to the poem, your answer cannot be 'wrong'.

Questions on *Football at Slack* *Marks*

1. How do each of the words 'plunging' and 'bareback' in line 1 help you to picture the scene where the football game is taking place?

   2

2. *(a)* Suggest one literary technique which is used in lines 2 and 3?

   1

   (b) What is the effect of this technique?

   2

3. What picture is suggested to you by each of the following:
   'ball jumped up' (line 4);
   'men spouted like water' (line 5).

   4

4. The poet uses a great deal of repetition in the first three stanzas. Suggest a reason for this.

   2

5. Stanza four describes the sky and the landscape. Explain in your own words how you picture the scene, paying particular attention to three of the following phrases:
   'fiery holes in heaven' (line 11);
   'Piled the hills' (line 12);
   'mad oils' (line 14);
   'the rain lowered a steel press' (line 15).

   6

6. Choose two words from stanza five and suggest how each one conveys to you the extreme wetness of the scene.

   4

7. Explain fully what you think the poet means by one of the following phrases:
   'world sank' (line 19);
   'valleys blued' (line 20).

   2

8. Describe fully in your own words the movements of the wingers and the movements of the goalie (lines 22–23).

   4

9. Would you call this poem 'romantic' or 'narrative' or 'descriptive'? Justify your answer by referring to details in the whole poem.

   3

Total Marks (30)

Under the Mountain

The poem *Under the Mountain* by Louis MacNeice is another descriptive poem. It also takes an unusual point of view or perspective of a scene. A first reading of the poem gives that much away — even the first line — 'seen from above'.

♦   Take a look at the whole poem first.

UNDER THE MOUNTAIN

Seen from above
The foam in the curving bay is a goose-quill
That feathers . . . unfeathers . . . itself.

Seen from above
5   The field is a flap and the haycocks buttons
To keep it flush with the earth

Seen from above
The house is a silent gadget whose purpose
Was a long since obsolete.

10   But when you get down
The breakers are cold scum and the wrack
Sizzles with stinking life.

When you get down
The field is a failed or a worth-while crop, the source
15   Of back-ache if not heartache.

And when you get down
The house is a maelstrom* of loves and hates where you —
Having got down — belong.

Louis MacNeice

*maelstrom — whirlpool

10

It is written in six stanzas. You can almost *see* a pattern or repetition in it. The first three stanzas all begin 'Seen from above'. Then the word 'But' in line 10 divides the poem in half. The next three stanzas begin 'when you get down'. It is worth looking at the structure of a poem because it could be significant in appreciating the overall meaning.

♦ Look at the first three stanzas. The first one is about a curving bay.

> Seen from above
> The foam in the curving bay is a goose-quill
> That feathers . . . unfeathers . . . itself.

It uses a metaphor suggesting that from above the foam of the sea looks like a curving goose-quill which 'feathers' and 'unfeathers' as the waves roll in. Why is this unusual image effective? Can you picture the colour of the waves and the texture — the soft whiteness like a feather? It also helps to picture the movement of the sea, in and out. Finally, it reminds us that from above, the sea would look flat like a feather.

In the second stanza, you should see another metaphor.

> Seen from above
> 5 The field is a flap and the haycocks buttons
> To keep it flush with the earth

A square field looks like a 'flap' or a pocket and the haycocks are like buttons holding it in place. This is effective because the field would be square like a patch of coloured cloth, possibly yellow. From above, the haycocks would look like flat buttons.

Then you might expect another metaphor in the third stanza.

> Seen from above
> The house is a silent gadget whose purpose
> Was long since obsolete.

This time a house is likened to a 'silent gadget'. This image is unusual and it might puzzle you. You might write your notes in question form. How can a house be like a gadget? Possibly, an odd shape — neither square nor round. Gadget suggests an instrument possibly of unknown purpose. But why silent? We think of houses as being full of people and noisy. But from above, a house would appear to be quiet. 'Obsolete' means out-of-date or of no further use. That, too, is puzzling at this stage in the poem and you may want to come back to the idea.

♦ Read again the second part of the poem beginning with 'But'.

> 10 But when you get down
> The breakers are cold scum and the wrack
> Sizzles with stinking life.

We know that 'but' can suggest a change of direction or a contrast. So try to note all the changes that you see. First of all, the word 'down'. The poet has come *down* to earth. We are no longer taking up a position in the sky.

11

Secondly, notice that the poet now says 'you'. The reader gets the feeling that he is being pulled down to look more closely at the details.

Thirdly, notice that the details are not pleasant ones. The words no longer have positive connotations or suggestions.

In the fourth stanza, note that he uses the words 'cold scum' and 'wrack'. Both scum and wrack suggest the messy debris that might be found at the edge of the sea. The word 'cold' also suggests that the sea is uninviting. This unpleasantness is continued with 'stinking life' which suggests that even the odour at the edge of the sea is unwelcoming. 'Sizzles' suggests the sound of the water at the sand's edge.

In the fifth stanza, as you would now expect, the field also appears unpleasant.

> When you get down
> The field is a failed or a worth-while crop, the source
> 15   Of back-ache if not heartache.

The poet suggests that the field is nothing but pain and failure for the farmer — 'back-ache' and 'heartache'. 'Heartache' particularly is a very strong, emotive word.

Finally, in the last stanza he describes the house.

> And when you get down
> The house is a maelstrom of loves and hates where you —
> Having got down — belong.

The word 'maelstrom' means whirlpool or storm — possibly a storm of emotions. This is supported by 'loves and hates', opposing emotions. A house is usually a scene of mixed emotions, turmoil, ups and downs. You should also notice the unusual punctuation in the last lines with the dashes around 'Having got down'. This makes this phrase parenthetical — but important. It emphasises this new position— *down*. This is where humans — we — belong — *down* on the earth, amongst the unpleasant as well as the pleasant.

♦   This might bring us to consider the ideas of the poem. Possibly viewed from above, the world does look almost ideal or perfect. The details, the smells, the unpleasantness cannot be experienced. Viewed from above or from an uninvolved position, the world is one-dimensional and devoid of emotions. A house does look like a 'gadget'. However, on the earth — when we are fully caught up with family, friends, school and work — all the realities are apparent and this is where we 'belong'.

But why is the poem called *Under the Mountain*? Your answer is as good as mine. You have to think about it.

Questions on *Under the Mountain*

Marks

1. Look at stanzas 1–2.

    (a) How does the poem link them? 1

    (b) What is the focus of attention in each of these stanzas? 3

    (c) In each stanza, how do three images each help you to picture the scene? 6

2. Look at stanzas 4–6.

    (a) 'But' is a word that can indicate a change in a poem. What change might be indicated here? 2

    (b) Choose three of the following words or phrases and say what each one tells you about the breakers:
    'cold scum (line 11);
    'the wrack' (line 11);
    'sizzles' (line 12);
    'stinking life' (line 12). 6

    (c) Choose two words from lines 14–15 which suggest a negative or unpleasant picture to you and say how each word does this. 4

3. Look back over the whole poem.

    (a) In your own words, explain what the last two lines mean. 2

    (b) Say how each of the following techniques helps you to understand the poem better:
    repetition;
    punctuation;
    point of view. 6

Total Marks (30)

NARRATIVE POEMS

The next poem is a narrative one — it tells a story. It does not tell you everything. Sometimes you have to put together parts of the story for yourself.

♦ Read the whole poem first.

THE FIFTH SENSE

A 65-year old Cypriot, Nicolis Loizou, was wounded by security forces early today. He was challenged twice; when he failed to answer, troops opened fire. A subsequent hospital examination showed that the man was deaf. News item, December 30th, 1957.

Lamps burn all the night
Here, where people must be watched and seen,
And I, a shepherd, Nicolis Loizou,
Wish for the dark, for I have been
5 Sure-footed in the dark, but now my sight
Stumbles among these beds, scattered white boulders,
As I lean towards my far slumbering house
With the night lying upon my shoulders.

My sight was always good,
10 Better than others, I could taste wine and bread
And name the field they spattered when the harvest
Broke. I could coil in the red
Scent of the fox out of a maze of wood
And grass. I could touch mist, I could touch breath.
15 But of my sharp senses I had only four.
The fifth one pinned me to my death.

The soldiers must have called
The word they needed: Halt. Not hearing it,
I was their failure, relaxed against the winter
20 Sky, the flag of their defeat.
With their five senses they could not have told
That I lacked one, and so they had to shoot.
They would fire at a rainbow if it had
A colour less than they were taught.

25 Christ said that when one sheep
Was lost, the rest meant nothing any more.
Here in this hospital, where others' breathing
Swings like a lantern in the polished floor
And squeezes those who cannot sleep,
30 O see how precious each thing is, how dear,
For I may never touch, smell, taste or see
Again, because I could not hear.

Patricia Beer

◆ Start with the title: ***The Fifth Sense***.

What are the five senses? You have to work your way through the poem to find out which one the poet names as *The Fifth Sense*.

◆ Where is the poem taking place?

> Lamps burn all the night
> *Here*, *where people must be watched and seen*,
> And I, a shepherd, Nicolis Loizou,
> Wish for the dark, for I have been
> 5 Sure-footed in the dark, but now my sight
> Stumbles *among these beds*, scattered white boulders,
> As I lean towards my far slumbering house
> With the night lying upon my shoulders.

Where is 'Here' in line two? First you find out that lamps have to burn all night. Then you find out that people must be observed all through the night. Then in line 6 you discover that there are beds here. You might guess by this point that 'here' is a hospital or infirmary.

◆ Who is the speaker in the poem? The 'I' in line three? You discover that he is a shepherd, Nicolis Loizou, and from the next few lines you work out that he might be a patient in the hospital. It sounds as if he is blind as he stumbles among beds.

The poet calls the beds 'scattered white boulders'. You should try to think why they might be described in that way, an unusual metaphor. Perhaps they are like the rocks on the hillside where the shepherd watched his sheep. The rocks could be large — as big as a bed and also white. The shepherd is comparing his movements on the hillside when he was sure-footed and confident to the way he now trips and stumbles around the beds in the hospital.

On the hill, the shepherd would be walking towards his house which may have been asleep as night was falling on the fields. You might want to remember the 'slumbering house' and 'night' which might become important later when you are thinking about the poem's theme.

♦   What change do you notice in the second stanza of the poem?

> My sight was always good,
> 10   Better than others, I could taste wine and bread
> And name the field they spattered when the harvest
> Broke. I could coil in the red
> Scent of the fox out of a maze of wood
> And grass. I could touch mist, I could touch breath.
> 15   But of my sharp senses I had only four.
> The fifth one pinned me to my death.

The speaker tells you about the past. He then tells you something about four of his five senses — how good each one was. His sight was always good; his sense of taste was so good that he could tell you which field the grapes and wheat came from to make the wine and bread. His sense of smell was so good that he could detect the odour of fox in the wood. Finally, he says — in an exaggerated way — that he could even touch mist.

You then find out which sense is missing when he has named four but left out the sense of hearing. He had four sharp senses but the fifth one 'pinned' him to his death. The poet is building up to a moment of drama in the poem by not actually naming the 'fifth sense'. Also the word 'pinned' is dramatic and even full of emotion. It sounds painful as if a fighter is pinning an enemy to the ground or a collector is pinning a butterfly to a board. And you also wonder why this deaf man was destined to die because he couldn't hear.

♦   The third stanza tells you about the incident.

> The soldiers must have called
> The word they needed: Halt. Not hearing it,
> I was their failure, relaxed against the winter
> 20   Sky, the flag of their defeat.
> With their five senses they could not have told
> That I lacked one, and so they had to shoot.
> They would fire at a rainbow if it had
> A colour less than they were taught.

Soldiers must have called to the shepherd to stop. Because he was deaf, he could not hear them shouting and he continued to move. The soldiers couldn't account for such disobedience. The poet uses a metaphor when he calls the shepherd 'the flag of their defeat'. They thought that the shepherd was being disobedient and they therefore had to shoot him. The poet is criticising the soldiers. He suggests that if they had been deaf they might have been more sensitive. They might have realised that the shepherd could not hear them. When it is stated that they would fire at a rainbow if it had one less colour then it should, he is suggesting that soldiers cannot afford to recognise individual differences. The tone of these lines is critical — almost cynical — about the soldiers' way of thinking.

♦ Finally, the last stanza takes us back to the hospital in the present time.

> 25 Christ said that when one sheep
> Was lost, the rest meant nothing any more.
> Here in this hospital, where others' breathing
> Swings like a lantern in the polished floor
> And squeezes those who cannot sleep,
> 30 O see how precious each thing is, how dear,
> For I may never touch, smell, taste or see
> Again, because I could not hear.

Why would the shepherd say that the breathing of other patients in the hospital 'swings like a lantern'? How could this metaphor be appropriate? Could it be that breathing is regular like the gentle swinging of a lantern might be regular, to and fro? This might seem to be appropriate because the shepherd cannot hear. So instead of saying that the breathing **sounds** like something regular, like the ticking of a clock, perhaps, he says that it is like **looking** at something regular — the swinging of a lantern. This seems an appropriate or effective image because it is a visual image and the shepherd is deaf.

♦ Finally, the ending of the poem is dramatic. There has been a regular rhyme throughout the poem, but at the end the rhyme of 'dear' and 'hear' makes these two words particularly important. It is also significant that the poet has not used the word 'hear' until this point. The title is 'The Fifth Sense'. The shepherd said that he had only four senses without saying which one in particular he was missing. Now the final important word of the poem is 'hear'. Also the sound of the last three lines is effective. The words are monosyllables — the list of 'touch, smell, taste or see'. The ending seems to hammer home the message of the poem.

We call a poem like this a dramatic monologue because it is one person speaking and telling us about himself at the same time that he is narrating a tale or exploring an idea. We learn a great deal about the shepherd. But the poem is also about soldiers and war. Wars are fought because men cannot accept differences between nations and peoples. Soldiers, particularly, are forced to demand uniformity; the enemy is the man who is different or who fails to conform. The shepherd was different.

Questions on *The Fifth Sense*

Marks

1. Look again at the place being described in stanza one (lines 1–8).

    (a) Explain why the lamps must burn all night.

    1

    (b) '... now my sight
    Stumbles among these beds, scattered white boulders,' (lines 5–6)
    Explain how the imagery in these lines helps you to picture the scene being described

    4

    (c) What do you think the speaker or shepherd means by 'my far slumbering house' (line 7)?

    2

2. Look again at stanza 2 (lines 9–16).

    (a) Explain, in your own words, how each of the shepherd's four senses was skilled or well-developed.

    4

    (b) Explain the importance of the word 'But' in line 15.

    2

    (c) What is the effect of using the word 'pinned' in line 16?

    2

3. Look again at stanza 3 (lines 17–24).

    (a) Explain in your own words what you think happened to the shepherd.

    3

    (b) Explain what is meant by 'the flag of their defeat' (line 20).

    2

    (c) What do the last two lines of this stanza (23–24) tell you about the soldiers? You should use your own words.

    2

    (d) What is the effect of using a 'rainbow' at this point in the poem?

    2

4. '... others' breathing
    Swings like a lantern in the polished floor ...' (lines 27–28).
    How effective do you find the image in these lines?

    2

5. Explain fully two ways in which the final lines (lines 31–32) are made dramatic. You may wish to consider:
    rhyme; rhythm; sound; title; structure.

    4

Total Marks (30)

The Man He Killed

Another poem which tells a story is *The Man He Killed*. It has a similar theme to *The Fifth Sense*.

♦ You can recognise immediately that the poem is not a modern one and it is not describing a modern setting.

THE MAN HE KILLED

'Had he and I but met
    By some old ancient inn,
We should have sat us down to wet
    Right many a nipperkin!*

5 'But ranged as infantry,
    And staring face to face,
I shot at him as he at me,
    And killed him in his place.

'I shot him dead because —
10   Because he was my foe,
Just so: my foe of course he was;
    That's clear enough; although

'He thought he'd 'list, perhaps,
    Off hand like — just as I —
15 Was out of work — had sold his traps —
    No other reason why.

'Yes; quaint and curious war is!
    You shoot a fellow down
You'd treat if met where any bar is,
20   Or help to half-a-crown.'

Thomas Hardy

*beer-mug

What are the clues? Some of the vocabulary is old-fashioned — or archaic — like 'nipperkin' or 'half-a-crown'. Even 'foe' we might call 'enemy' and 'ancient inn' a pub or hotel.

♦   First identify the speaker in the poem. Probably a young man who enlisted in the war. He guesses that the man he shot was probably like him — enlisting in the war because he was out of work. The man he shot seemed to be a hunter or a trapper.

♦   Is this poem a dramatic monologue? It does seem to be one man speaking and telling us about himself, his situation and also conveying the ideas of the poem.

♦   What is the situation?

> 'Had he and I but met
>> By some old ancient inn,
> We should have sat us down to wet
>> Right many a nipperkin!*

> 5 'But ranged as infantry,
>> And staring face to face,
> I shot at him as he at me,
>> And killed him in his place.

The young man is speculating about the man he has just killed. He says that if the two of them had met under different circumstances, they probably would have set themselves down to have a drink together. However, instead they met as soldiers staring at each other 'face to face'. They shoot each other because they are enemies and the speaker kills the other soldier.

♦   In stanzas three and four, he reflects on why he killed the man: 'he was my foe' — the enemy.

> 'I shot him dead because —
> 10   Because he was my foe,
> Just so: my foe of course he was;
>> That's clear enough; although

> 'He thought he'd 'list, perhaps,
>> Off hand like — just as I —
> 15 Was out of work — had sold his traps —
>> No other reason why.

Why do you think he repeats this phrase 'my foe' and also emphasises it with 'of course'? This seems to emphasise his uncertainty or even fear about what he has done. The rhyme in this stanza also emphasises the word 'foe', rhyming with 'so' and 'although'.

This stanza carries on to the next with the run-on line or enjambment and the details in this stanza emphasise the similarities between the two men or enemies.

- Finally, the last stanza is the speaker's reflection on war.

> 'Yes; quaint and curious war is!
> You shoot a fellow down
> You'd treat if met where any bar is,
> 20   Or help to half-a-crown.'

The exclamation suggests that the statement is emotive. He is saying how odd it is that you kill a man in war who you would be friendly with in a bar.

In some ways, the idea in this poem is similar to the one in *The Fifth Sense*. The enemy is the man on the other side and the hostility or enmity might not even make much sense. The two enemies seem to be more alike than different, but by circumstances they are pitted 'face to face'.

Questions on *The Man He Killed*

Marks

1. Explain how one example of word choice and one example of sentence structure in stanza one (lines 1–4) suggests that the events in this poem took place many years ago.

    4

2. Explain fully the effect of the word 'But' (line 5).

    3

3. What effect do you think the rhyme has on the opening of this tale?

    2

4. Look again at the poetic techniques used in stanza three (lines 9–12). Explain how three of the following are used effectively in telling the story:
    repetition;
    rhyme;
    punctuation;
    enjambment.

    6

5. In stanza 4 (lines 13–16), in speaking about the man he killed, the poet tells us about himself.
    What do you learn about him in this stanza?

    4

6. Give a reason for the punctuation in line 17.

    2

7. Explain in your own words what is 'quaint and curious' about war.

    4

8. What is the effect of the poem looking like direct speech?

    2

9. How effective do you find the title to the poem?

    3

Total Marks (30)

THEMES IN POETRY

ASPECTS OF GROWING UP

The last two poems had a similar theme — about war and recognising the enemy. A number of poems which you have studied already are probably about growing up. The next four poems examine aspects of growing up. However, the ideas on that topic are very different. You cannot state a theme properly with one or two words, like 'growing up'. Try with each of the following poems to define the themes in as much detail as possible.

♦ Read *In Mrs Tilscher's Class*, trying to get an idea of the situation.

IN MRS TILSCHER'S CLASS

You could travel up the Blue Nile
with your finger, tracing the route
while Mrs Tilscher chanted the scenery.
Tana. Ethiopia. Khartoum. Aswan.
5   That for an hour, then a skittle of milk
and the chalky Pyramids rubbed into dust.
A window opened with a long pole.
The laugh of a bell swung by a running child.

This was better than home. Enthralling books.
10 The classroom glowed like a sweetshop.
Sugar paper. Coloured shapes. Brady and Hindley
faded, like the faint, uneasy smudge of a mistake.
Mrs Tilscher loved you. Some mornings, you found
she'd left a good gold star by your name.
15 The scent of a pencil slowly, carefully, shaved.
A xylophone's nonsense heard from another form.

Over the Easter term, the inky tadpoles changed
from commas into exclamation marks. Three frogs
hopped in the playground, freed by a dunce,
20 followed by a line of kids, jumping and croaking
away from the lunch queue. A rough boy
told you how you were born. You kicked him, but stared
at your parents, appalled, when you got back home.

That feverish July, the air tasted of electricity.
25 A tangible alarm made you always untidy, hot,
fractious under the heavy, sexy sky. You asked her
how you were born and Mrs Tilscher smiled,
then turned away. Reports were handed out.
You ran through the gates, impatient to be grown,
30 as the sky split open into a thunderstorm.

Carol Ann Duffy

The situation seems to be a primary school classroom and a young girl seems to be learning about geography in the first stanza.

> You could travel up the Blue Nile
> with your finger, tracing the route
> while Mrs Tilscher chanted the scenery.
> Tana. Ethiopia. Khartoum. Aswan.
> 5   That for an hour, then a skittle of milk
> and the chalky Pyramids rubbed into dust.
> A window opened with a long pole.
> The laugh of a bell swung by a running child.

A number of the details suggest the happy mood or atmosphere of the classroom. The teacher Mrs Tilscher 'chanted' the names of the places. The pupils then have a break with a 'skittle of milk'. The speaker also mentions chalk, dust, the window pole and the bell. The nature of these details make the scene seem a peaceful, secure, well-known one. Even the sound of the bell is described as a 'laugh'. A running child suggests happiness and freedom.

♦   The second stanza continues this happy atmosphere.

> This was better than home. Enthralling books.
> 10   The classroom glowed like a sweetshop.
> Sugar paper. Coloured shapes. Brady and Hindley
> faded, like the faint, uneasy smudge of a mistake.
> Mrs Tilscher loved you. Some mornings, you found
> she'd left a good gold star by your name.
> 15   The scent of a pencil slowly, carefully, shaved.
> A xylophone's nonsense heard from another form.

What details are used here which seem pleasant? Think of details which appeal to your senses. Sight? Enthralling books and a glowing classroom and coloured shapes. Taste? Sweetshop and perhaps even sugar. Smell? Scent of a pencil. Sound? A xylophone. Other details are often appealing. 'Mrs Tilscher loved you' and 'a gold star'.

Is there anything in this stanza which seems negative or unpleasant or even out-of-place? Brady and Hindley were child murderers. A mention of them seems unusual. The line which follows also has negative suggestions with words like 'faded' compared to the colourful shapes and the glow of the classroom. The phrase 'faint, uneasy, smudge of a mistake' also has a sinister suggestion of something gone wrong.

♦ Stanza three deals with change.

> Over the Easter term, the inky tadpoles changed
> from commas into exclamation marks. Three frogs
> hopped in the playground, freed by a dunce,
> 20 followed by a line of kids, jumping and croaking
> away from the lunch queue. A rough boy
> told you how you were born. You kicked him, but stared
> at your parents, appalled, when you got back home.

How does the poet describe the change in the tadpoles? What figure of speech does she use? Does it seem effective? A small tadpole would look like a comma, in shape and in colour. If a comma 'stretches', it becomes an exclamation point which suggests change, drama or surprise. The details which follow emphasise this idea of surprise and drama. Frogs hopping, freed by a stupid boy, and kids jumping and imitating the frogs. Finally, a rough boy does the most dramatic thing when he tells the speaker how she was born. 'Stared' and 'appalled' suggest that the girl is shocked by the new knowledge.

♦ At the end, more words and details suggest that the girl is changing or learning about life.

> That feverish July, the air tasted of electricity.
> 25 A tangible alarm made you always untidy, hot,
> fractious under the heavy, sexy sky. You asked her
> how you were born and Mrs Tilscher smiled,
> then turned away. Reports were handed out.
> You ran through the gates, impatient to be grown,
> 30 as the sky split open into a thunderstorm.

The atmosphere of a hot July full of electricity is appropriate. The weather is thundery under a 'hot' and 'heavy, sexy sky'. In the last line, the splitting open of sky suggests a dramatic thunderstorm. And Mrs Tilscher doesn't tell her how she was born.

Yes, the theme could be said to be growing up. The open gates might suggest the entrance to adolescence from childhood. The girl is 'impatient to be grown' but an idea of the poem is that growing up is at times painful, uncomfortable, and even shocking.

Questions on *In Mrs Tilscher's Class*

Marks

1. *(a)* Why might the subject being taught by Mrs Tilscher (lines 1–4) be appropriate to the theme of this poem? **1**

    (b) Show how the word choice in these lines suggests how Mrs Tilscher teaches her subject. **2**

2. Explain fully the way the poet makes line 4 significant. **2**

3. Choose three of the details in lines 5–8 and explain what each one suggests about the scene. **6**

4. Explain how the speaker shows her attitude to school in lines 9–11. You should consider one example of word choice and one example of imagery. **4**

5. How do the senses evoke memories of these early school days in lines 14–16? You should refer to at least three senses. **3**

6. Change takes place over the Easter term (lines 17–23). How does the speaker show this change in these lines? You should consider one example of word choice and one of imagery. **4**

7. Look again at line 24 to the end of the poem.

    (a) Show how two words from these lines each suggests that the speaker is no longer as happy and secure as she was before Easter. **2**

    (b) What does the child's question (lines 27–28) suggest about the change in her? **2**

    (c) What do the final two lines of the poem suggest to you about the speaker's development? You should comment on word choice or imagery in these lines. **4**

Total Marks (30)

Childhood is also about aspects of growing up.

♦ First, just look at the poem.

CHILDHOOD

Long time he lay upon the sunny hill,
    To his father's house below securely bound.
Far off the silent, changing sound was still,
    With the black islands lying thick around.

5 He saw each separate height, each vaguer hue,
    Where the massed islands rolled in mist away,
And though all ran together in his view
    He knew that unseen straits between them lay.

Often he wondered what new shores were there.
10   In thought he saw the still light on the sand,
The shallow water clear in tranquil air,
    And walked through it in joy from strand to strand.

Over the sound a ship so slow would pass
    That in the black hill's gloom it seemed to lie.
15 The evening sound was smooth like sunken glass,
    And time seemed finished ere the ship passed by.

Grey tiny rocks slept round him where he lay,
    Moveless as they, more still as evening came,
The grasses threw straight shadows far away,
20   And from the house his mother called his name.

Edwin Muir

What do you notice? Four-line stanzas, regular rhyme, mostly one syllable.

♦ Then look at key words in the poem. Are they positive or negative? Pleasant or unpleasant?

> Long time he lay upon the sunny hill,
>> To his father's house below securely bound.
> Far off the silent, changing sound was still,
>> With the black islands lying thick around.

The first stanza sounds secure and happy with words like 'sunny' and 'securely bound'. However, the silence and the word 'black' suggest that the distant view is ominous or unknown.

This mixed sense is continued in the next stanza, perhaps slightly more ominously. The distance is vague and mist-like. The 'unseen straits' sound as if they could be dangerous.

> 5　He saw each separate height, each vaguer hue,
>> Where the massed islands rolled in mist away,
> And though all ran together in his view
>> He knew that unseen straits between them lay.

However, in stanza three, the tranquillity is continued with 'still light' and 'tranquil air'. He even uses the word 'joy'.

> Often he wondered what new shores were there.
> 10　　In thought he saw the still light on the sand,
> The shallow water clear in tranquil air,
>> And walked through it in joy from strand to strand.

♦ Read stanza four aloud.

> Over the sound a ship so slow would pass
>> That in the black hill's gloom it seemed to lie.
> 15　The evening sound was smooth like sunken glass,
>> And time seemed finished ere the ship passed by.

Do you notice anything unusual in this stanza? Does it sound different? The poet uses the word 'slow' and the number of long vowels — o, a, and u — make these lines read slowly. The alliteration in the first line of the 's' sound also draws attention to these words and to the fact that a ship was moving slowly and silent on the horizon. Words like 'black' and 'gloom' and even 'evening' suggest the changing of time — and even the atmosphere.

You might be thinking that the poet is writing about the passage of time which in childhood seems unbelievably slow. Sometimes the change, like the passage of the ship, is so slow that it seems imperceptible or unnoticeable. The mood or time of the poem seems also to have changed. The first stanza on the sunny hill seems like morning. This fourth stanza suggests evening. The poem seems to be using time of day to suggest the change in the life of the young boy.

♦   The last stanza is the most suggestive of all.

> Grey tiny rocks slept round him where he lay,
>   Moveless as they, more still as evening came,
> The grasses threw straight shadows far away,
> 20   And from the house his mother called his name.

The rocks are 'grey' and 'tiny'. Both adjectives suggest that the rocks could be hidden. The other detail of the stanza is also vague or uncertain with grasses throwing 'shadows'. Long, straight shadows suggest the end of the day when shadows are lengthening.

♦   The final line, however, recalls us to the initial situation at the start of the poem. From his home his mother is calling him.

This seems to be about a young boy who is moving slowly — seeming not to be moving at all really — away from his home. He seems to be thinking about the distance which is still vague and unknown. The water and the mention of islands suggests that his journey to the distance will involve change, a journey that will make a real difference, like moving from one island to another. It is the poem's title which confirms that this poem is probably describing the last moments of childhood security and happiness.

Yes, the poem is about growing up again, but it is different from the last poem. It is about gradual change — not sudden — and it is also about the vagueness and uncertainty of the future.

Questions on *Childhood*

Marks

1. Describe the situation presented in the first stanza.   2

2. *(a)* How does the poet establish a mood in the first two lines of the poem? You should consider word choice and sentence structure.   2

    (b) What contrast to lines 1–2 is suggested by the details of lines 3–4?   4

3. Explain in your own words how the boy's view (lines 7–8) is different from reality.   2

4. Read again stanza 3 (lines 9–12). Explain how two words or phrases each suggests the child's attitude to the distant view.   4

5. Show how the poet creates the impression of the slow passage of time through three of the following techniques in stanzas one to four (lines 1–16):
    sound;
    imagery;
    rhyme and rhythm;
    sentence structure.   6

6. Show how two details in lines 17–19 create the mood at this point in the poem?   4

7. What effect does the final line of the poem have upon its meaning?   2

8. The title of the poem suggests that the poet is writing about more than the view from the hill.
    Explain what else you think the poet may be considering in this poem.   4

Total Marks
                (30)

The third poem about childhood, by Carol Ann Duffy, is called *Late* and is an unusual one.

LATE

She was eight. She was out late.
She bounced a tennis ball homewards before her in the last of the light.
She'd been warned. She'd been told. It grew cold.
She took a shortcut through the churchyard.
5   She was a small child making her way home. She was quite brave.
She fell into an open grave.

It was deep. It was damp. It smelled strange.
Help, she cried, *Help, it's Me*! She shouted her own name.
Nobody came.
10 The church bells tolled sadly. Shame. Shame.

She froze. She had a blue nose.
She clapped her hands.
She stamped her feet in soft, slip-away soil.
She hugged herself. Her breath was a ghost floating up from a grave.
15 Then she prayed.

But only the moon stared down with its callous face.
Only the spiteful stars sniggered, far out in space.
Only the gathering clouds threw down a clap of thunder like an ace.
And her, she was eight, going on nine.
20 She was late.

Carol Ann Duffy

After reading the poem through, say what you think is different about this poem. You might comment on a number of things orally this time before writing down answers to questions.

♦ Which do you think is the most unusual feature? The situation? The sound? The unusual word choice and imagery? The sentence structures?

♦ What is the situation? The poem seems to be about a young girl of eight who is bouncing a ball home late one afternoon when she had been warned to come home earlier. She takes a shortcut through a churchyard or graveyard of all places.

♦ How does the poet use sound to reinforce the situation and the ideas of the poem? Does the sound, with the frequent rhymes, make it seem as if she is bouncing a ball? 'Eight' and 'gate', 'told' and 'cold', 'brave' and 'grave'.

♦ What kind of words does the poet use? Pleasant sensations or unpleasant? The words 'cold' and 'churchyard' and the darkness suggest the dangers. The details also appeal to the senses. The darkness, the dampness, her shouting, the silence, the church bells. The first stanza ends in a climax when she falls into a grave which, of course, suggests death.

♦ What type of sentences are used? Does the number of short simple sentences make the situation even more dramatic? Her shouts are italicised words to make them stand out. Why do you think she shouts her own name?

♦ How does the poet make 'Nobody came' more dramatic?

♦ Why do you think that 'Shame' is repeated?

♦ The poet uses the image that her 'breath was a ghost'. Do you think that is an appropriate image? How can breath be like a ghost?

♦ At the end of the poem the moon is personified — it sounds like a person staring down at the girl in the grave. Does anyone or anything take any notice of the girl's situation? The words 'stared' and 'callous' suggests that the moon is uncaring about the little girl's plight. The stars also sound unhelpful: they are 'spiteful' and they 'sniggered' and they are distant — 'far out in space'. The only response to the little girl's plight comes from the clouds which throw down a clap of thunder 'like an ace' which makes the situation more dangerous.

♦ Do you think that the ending of the poem is effective? It ends simply and dramatically, emphasising her youth and then repeating the important line of the poem: 'She was late.'

♦ The poem is puzzling. What is it about? A little girl growing up too soon because she accidentally stumbles upon reality or death? Is she forced to face up to danger and reality when she is only eight?

The poem is unusual because the poet seems to make a serious subject almost sound like fun. The poem is like a surprise.

Growing up? It does seem to be about that. Growing up accidentally when very young. The loneliness, fear and isolation is an important part of the way the theme is expressed in this poem. The rest of the world — and even the natural world — seems not to care a jot about the little girl's plight.

Questions on *Late*

Marks

1. The first three lines suggest that there is danger. What possible dangers can you see in the situation?

   2

2. What do you find unusual about the first stanza (lines 1–6) of this poem? Comment on each of the following and give an example:

   (a) rhyme;

   (b) rhythm;

   (c) sound.

   6

3. How does the poet create a climax in the first stanza?

   2

4. What unusual features do you see in stanza two (lines 7–10)? Comment on any two of the lines. You may wish to comment on such features as sentence structure, punctuation, or repetition.

   (a) It was deep. It was damp. It smelled strange.

   (b) *Help*, she cried, *Help, it's Me!* She shouted her own name.

   (c) Nobody came.

   (d) The church bells tolled sadly. Shame. Shame.

   4

5. *(a)* What words or details in stanza three (lines 11–15) make the situation sound unpleasant? Choose two and explain fully in each case.

   4

   (b) What image does the poet use in this same stanza? How effective do you find it in helping to create atmosphere?

   3

6. What change do you see with the word "But" in line 16?

   2

7. Comment on any two of these details from the last stanza and say how each helps to express the young girl's situation:

   (a) the moon;

   (b) the stars;

   (c) the clouds;

   (d) the thunder

   4

8. What do you think this poem is really about? Give your own ideas but support them by referring to details of the poem.

   3

Total marks (30)

POEMS ABOUT WEATHER

Sometimes poets use weather to say something about the way people live or the type of relationships they make. In other words, weather is used as a metaphor, a device for helping to express themes or ideas.

You may have read the poem *Stopping by Woods* by Robert Frost which uses a snowy scene to suggest attitudes to life. Or *Wind* by Theodore Roethke which tells about a young child's fears when isolated on top of a greenhouse. Ted Hughes also has a poem called *Wind* which uses a storm to describe feelings of insecurity.

This poem, *Storm on the Island* by Seamus Heaney, is similar in some ways. This poem is perhaps more difficult than some of the earlier poems you have looked at in this book, but it is a thought-provoking poem and worth the effort.

STORM ON THE ISLAND

We are prepared: we build our houses squat,
Sink walls in rock and roof them with good slate.
This wizened earth has never troubled us
With hay, so, as you see, there are no stacks
5 Or stooks that can be lost. Nor are there trees
Which might prove company when it blows full
Blast: you know what I mean — leaves and branches
Can raise a tragic chorus in a gale
So that you listen to the thing you fear
10 Forgetting that it pummels your house too.
But there are no trees, no natural shelter.
You might think that the sea is company,
Exploding comfortably down on the cliffs
But no: when it begins, the flung spray hits
15 The very windows, spits like a tame cat
Turned savage. We just sit tight while wind dives
And strafes invisibly. Space is a salvo,
We are bombarded by the empty air.
Strange, it is a huge nothing that we fear.

Seamus Heaney

♦ In the first stanza of the poem, 'We' suggests that the speaker of the poem is not alone. With someone else, preparations are taken to make the home secure against the storm. Houses are small and low, built into the rocky hillside and slated well. The poem also describes a rather grim landscape. The word 'wizened' suggests that not much grows on this island; it seems old and dried up — not fertile. There are no hay stacks or stooks which could be blown away — probably because the ground could not grow long grass. There are no trees either so the landscape seems very bleak and barren.

♦ In this barren landscape, the poet suggests that there are no natural features of the landscape which provide any comfort or company. There are no trees to 'prove company' in a full storm. He uses personification to suggest that the branches of the trees might be a chorus — albeit a tragic one — in the sounds that they could make in a gale. He uses the word 'pummels' to suggest that the storm is like a fight or a punch-up.

♦ The other natural feature which might be company is the sea. The phrase 'Exploding comfortably' is an oxymoron; it seems to be a combination of opposites. How can something explode comfortably? The sea spray is made to sound like a spitting cat. That phrase also seems to be an oxymoron — 'spits like a tame cat'. These two phrases suggest that the power of the sea can turn savage. It might have been company, but it can turn against the inhabitants of the house.

♦ The end of the poem says that the people 'just sit tight' in the storm. These three words even sound tight and nervous with the clipped sound of the final t's and the narrow 'i' vowel. The words 'vies and strafes' reminds us of the pummelling punch-up earlier in the poem. And 'bombarded' suggests warfare.

♦ The final line of the poem and the final oxymoron 'huge nothing' are revealing. How can you have a huge nothing? That seems like a contradiction in terms. What do we fear then? He suggests that we are afraid of something that is not even there.

♦ Go back to the title. Why is the storm on an island? A storm on an island would be worse because it is vulnerable — surrounded by the sea. It also suggests isolation. The words 'we' and 'company' are repeated suggesting the importance of companionship.

♦ A storm is, of course, a physical force, but it can also be an emotional force or a stress. It could represent life's troubles like death or loss or separation. You could say that the poet uses the storm and the island as a central metaphor for the poem. Heaney *extends* the metaphor throughout the poem.

Questions on *Storm on the Island*

Marks

1. What does the word 'we' tell you about the speaker in the poem?   1

2. Explain briefly two ways in which the speaker of the poem is 'prepared' from your reading of lines 1–2.   2

3. How does the word choice in lines 3–5 help you to picture the type of landscape being described in this poem.   2

4. Explain in your own words how the speaker suggests that trees can 'prove company' in a storm in lines 6–10.   2

5. What does the word 'pummels' (line 10) suggest to you about the wind?   2

6. Look again at the way the sea is described in lines 12–16.

   (a) What is unusual about the phrase 'exploding comfortably' (line 13)?   2

   (b) Comment fully on how effective you find the speaker's description of the sea. You should consider word choice and figures of speech.   4

7. What is suggested by the use of the word 'bombarded' in line 18?   2

8. What is unusual about the final line? You should consider two of the   2
   following:
   > sentence structure;
   > word choice;
   > oxymoron.   4

9. Suggest two places in the poem where you think sound contributes to meaning.   4

10. Now explain fully what significance you think the title may have.   3

Total Marks   (30)

Another poem about weather is *Rain* by Robert Crawford. Tone is important in this poem. Tone is the author's attitude to his subject. The tone suggests that you don't want to take this poem too seriously.

As you read the poem, try to imagine the way you think that the poet would be saying it. Which words might he emphasise? What tone of voice might he use?

RAIN

A motorbike breaks down near Sanna in torrential rain,
Pouring loud enough to perforate limousines, long enough
To wash us to Belize. Partick's
Fish-scaled with wetness. Drips shower from foliage, cobbles, tourists
5   From New York and Dusseldorf at the tideline
Shoes lost in bogs, soaked in potholes, clarted with glaur.
And old woman is splashed by a bus. A gash
In cloud. Indians
Arrived this week to join their families and who do not feel
10   Scottish one inch push onwards into a drizzle
That gets heavy and vertical. Golf umbrellas
Come up like orchids on fast-forward film; exotic
Cagoules fluoresce nowhere, speckling a hillside, and plump.
Off dykes and gutters, overflowing
15   Ditches, a granary of water drenches the shoulders
Of Goatfell and Schiehallion. Maps under Perspex go bleary,
Spectacles clog, Strathclyde, Tayside, Dundee
Catch it, fingers spilling with water, oil-stained
As it comes down in sheets, blows
20   Where there are no trees, snow-set. Without thought of the morrow.
Weddings, prunes, abattoirs, strippers, Glen Nevis, snails
Blur in its democracy, down your back, on your breasts.
In Kilmarnock a child walks naked. A woman laughs.
In cars, in Tiree bedrooms, in caravans and tenements,
25   Couples sleeved in love, the gibbous Govan rain.

Robert Crawford

- In the first line this is a key word 'rain' which is also the title of the poem. The rain is also said to be 'torrential' which seems a very dramatic sort of word.

- The exaggeration in the next few lines is another hint about the poet's tone or attitude. The rain is further dramatised or exaggerated when the poet says that the rain was 'loud enough' to perforate the limousines. The rain is pictured like long sharp nails going through the roof of cars like a nail would perforate the lid of a jam jar. It is also 'long enough' to wash you to Belize.

- The originality of the images in the next few lines continues the exaggeration. The poet suggests that the country has never been so wet. Partick is 'fish-scaled' with rain. We often say in Scotland we have webbed feet — the same kind of idea.

- A whole list of wetness follows. 'Shoes lost in bogs . . .'

- finishing with the Scottish dialect 'clarted with glaur'.

- The original images continue. 'A gash in clouds' is an image which makes it sound as if someone has stuck a giant knife into the billowy, dark thunderclouds to release the watery contents.

- When the poet talks about golf umbrellas in line 11 the mood seems even lighter or more cheerful. The simile makes the colourful umbrellas sound like beautiful orchids opening quickly. The cagoules are also colourful and all this brightness dots the hillside. The mood in this part of the poem seems cheerful or even happy despite the rain because of the words and images which the poet uses.

- The scene becomes increasingly vivid.

- The list runs over in lines 11–16.

- The mountains are personified with water dripping off their shoulders in lines 15–16.

- The phrase 'Blur in its democracy' (line 22) is an unusual one and stands out in this descriptive poem. Democracy means that everyone is equal. Could this suggest that the rain falls on every person regardless of class, colour or religion?

The poem is not difficult once you get used to some of its features of exaggeration, long lists, strange details, Scottish place names and colloquial words — perhaps to suggest that rain is a key feature of Scottish life. The poet's tone is important. It seems humorous or even tongue-in-cheek — probably because humour is the only way to deal with rain, particularly in the west of Scotland.

Questions on *Rain*

Marks

1. How does the poet make the idea of rain seem important in the first line of the poem?

    2

2. Explain how exaggeration is used in lines 2–3 to emphasise further the rainy conditions.

    4

3. Explain in your own words what you think the poet means by 'Partick's / Fish-scaled with wetness.' (lines 3–4).

    2

4. Commenting on two of the details in the list in lines 4–6, show what effect you think the poet achieves with each.

    4

5. What do you think the poet means by the image 'A gash / In cloud' (lines 7–8)?

    2

6. What mood does the poet suggest to you by the details used in lines 11–21? You should comment on at least one example of word choice and one example of imagery to support your comment.

    5

7. Suggest how two of the following poetic techniques are used in lines 11–21 to create a vivid impression of the scene:
    personification;
    imagery;
    line structure;
    word choice.

    4

8. What do you think the poet means by the phrase 'Blur in its democracy' (line 22)?

    2

9. Choose two of the following techniques and say why you think they are the ones the poet uses to greatest effect in *Rain*:
    listing;
    structure of poem;
    place names;
    Scottish words.

    5

Total Marks (30)

TONE IN POETRY

Tone was important in the last poem, *Rain*.

Detecting tone is an important part of life — as well as in textual analysis. For example, someone may say to you, 'You really are a genius, aren't you?' You want to be pretty sure that you pick up on the tone. You would feel fairly silly taking seriously a comment which was meant in jest.

It is perhaps more difficult in poetry to detect the tone than in real life. Many of us are expecting poems to be serious or romantic and we might miss the mocking, humorous, sarcastic or tongue-in-cheek style of some poetry.

When you study a poem, you are often trying to understand an author's attitude towards his subject. There are lots of techniques that may give you clues to the author's attitude. Obviously, the words he uses are important. If they are pleasant words, they give a positive sense to the tone. If they are unpleasant or unsympathetic words, the poet's tone is probably negative.

Tone can be conveyed in ways other than word choice. For example, a short, simple sentence can make a comment humorous. Or exaggeration or unusual images can be humorous or even mocking — like saying that someone is 'fish-scaled'. Even punctuation can suggest a tone. Perhaps words in parenthesis might be adding a funny aside — or a sarcastic comment.

When we want to make fun of someone we sometimes imitate what they say or the way they say it. So words in quotation marks might be included to be mocking or perhaps the words might be colloquial or slang which is another way of showing tone or attitude toward a subject — the way Robert Crawford used 'clarted with glaur' in *Rain*.

Details in a poem might be so unusual that they are funny in the extreme.

The next two poems use a number of these ways of establishing their attitude toward a subject or tone.

One poem with a strange tone is *Stealing*. It also seems like a conversation between two people — as if the speaker of the poem is being asked questions — perhaps by some kind of counsellor or social worker.

Try to imagine the relationship between the two people, and particularly the attitude of the person speaking, as you read the poem for the first time.

STEALING

The most unusual thing I ever stole? A snowman.
Midnight. He looked magnificent; a tall, white mute
beneath the winter moon. I wanted him, a mate
with a mind as cold as the slice of ice
5   within my own brain. I started with the head.

Better off dead than giving in, not taking
what you want. He weighed a ton, his torso,
frozen stiff, hugged to my chest, a fierce chill
piercing my gut. Part of the thrill was knowing
10   that children would cry in the morning. Life's tough.

Sometimes I steal things I don't need. I joy-ride cars
to nowhere, break into houses just to have a look.
I'm a mucky ghost, leave a mess, maybe pinch a camera.
I watch my gloved hand twisting the doorknob.
15   A stranger's bedroom. Mirrors. I sigh like this. — *Aah.*

It took some time. Reassembled in the yard,
he didn't look the same. I took a run
and booted him. Again. Again. My breath ripped out
in rage. It seems daft now. Then I was standing
20   alone amongst lumps of snow, sick of the world.

Boredom. Mostly I'm so bored I could eat myself.
One time, I stole a guitar and thought I might
learn to play. I nicked a bust of Shakespeare once,
flogged it, but the snowman was strangest.
25   You don't understand a word I'm saying, do you?

Carol Ann Duffy

♦ The first stanza again seems to start in the middle of a conversation.

> The most unusual thing I ever stole? A snowman.
> Midnight. He looked magnificent; a tall, white mute
> beneath the winter moon. I wanted him, a mate
> with a mind as cold as the slice of ice
> 5 within my own brain. I started with the head.

What question do you imagine that the counsellor or the interviewer asked the person in the poem? The speaker answers 'A snowman'. The single word sentence 'Midnight' makes the theft even more dramatic. The alliteration of 'm' in magnificent, mute, moon, mate and mind draws attention to the description and sets the scene. There is something ominous about the image in line 4 — 'a mind as cold as a slice of ice'. The sound of the phrase is also interesting. The last sentence is, of course, dramatic.

♦ There is also something ominous about the way the speaker describes the snowman's theft in the second stanza.

> Better off dead than giving in, not taking
> what you want. He weighed a ton, his torso,
> frozen stiff, hugged to my chest, a fierce chill
> piercing my gut. Part of the thrill was knowing
> 10 that children would cry in the morning. Life's tough.

Removing the head, carrying the body, the phrases 'a fierce chill' and 'piercing my gut' suggests extreme pain and horror. Which idea do you find most shocking? For me, it is the idea that someone could be thrilled by children crying.

♦ The speaker goes on to elaborate about the things which he or she steals.

> Sometimes I steal things I don't need. I joy-ride cars
> to nowhere, break into houses just to have a look.
> I'm a mucky ghost, leave a mess, maybe pinch a camera.
> I watch my gloved hand twisting the doorknob.
> 15 A stranger's bedroom. Mirrors. I sigh like this. — *Aah*.

The slang words used 'joy-ride' and 'pinch' and 'mucky' suggests the casual callousness of the thefts. The gloved hand, the stranger's bedroom, the mirrors and the sigh are eerie. Why does the speaker do these things?

◆ The fourth stanza probably tells the most about the speaker's attitude or tone.

> It took some time. Reassembled in the yard,
> he didn't look the same. I took a run
> and booted him. Again. Again. My breath ripped out
> in rage. It seems daft now. Then I was standing
> 20 alone amongst lumps of snow, sick of the world.

He or she is frustrated and dissatisfied with the theft — booting the rebuilt snowman. The repeated word 'Again' confirms the anger and frustration as does the strong phrase 'ripped out in rage' to suggest the way the thief could hardly breathe with anger. 'Alone' and 'sick of the world' are even more obvious signs of emotional pain. We may not understand the speaker, but we are learning a great deal about his character.

◆ The last stanza tries to suggest a reason for actions and thefts.

> Boredom. Mostly I'm so bored I could eat myself.
> One time, I stole a guitar and thought I might
> learn to play. I nicked a bust of Shakespeare once,
> flogged it, but the snowman was strangest.
> 25 You don't understand a word I'm saying, do you?

Boredom. The single-word sentence and the exaggeration which follows suggest the speaker's attitude. The slang words 'nicked' and 'flogged' suggest the casual attitude toward the thefts. What do you find unusual about the last stolen items?

The final question suggests the speaker's attitude toward the questioner — the distance between them has not lessened during the conversation or interview. The question reminds us of the situation which was introduced in the first line of the poem. Do you feel after reading this poem that you know what kind of person is speaking and what kind of tone is being used? Or do you find that 'you don't understand a word'?

Questions on *Stealing*

Marks

1. Comment on two features of the first line which strike you as strange.
   2

2. How do two details in lines 2–3 help to establish a mood in the poem?
   4

3. *(a)* What does the figure of speech in line 4 tell you about the kind of person speaking?
   3

   (b) Stanza 2 (lines 6–10) tells much more about the person in the poem. By referring to two specific words or phrases, explain even more fully what kind of person is speaking?
   4

4. 'Sometimes I steal things I don't need.' (line 11).
   Show one way in which this comment is reinforced in this stanza (lines 11–15).
   2

5. Explain fully why you think the poet 'booted him' (line 18).
   2

6. Language techniques reveal even more about this person's stealing. By commenting on three of the following techniques, explain how the language used reveals the speaker's attitude or tone in stanzas 4 and 5 (lines 16–25):
   colloquial language;
   sentence structure;
   exaggeration;
   word choice.
   6

7. The final stanza (lines 21–25) reminds us of the situation also suggested by the first line of the poem. What do you think the situation might be and do you think it may have changed during this monologue?
   4

8. The title of the poem is *Stealing*, but the thefts seem pointless. To what extent do you think the poem is about stealing — or to what extent is it about something else?
   3

Total Marks (30)

In *The Grimm Sisters*, Liz Lochhead treats her subject humorously but yet she expresses some strong opinions.

Read the poem, trying to hear the tone even on a first reading.

THE GRIMM SISTERS

And for special things
(weddings, school-
concerts) the grown up girls next door
would do my hair.

5   Luxembourg announced Amami Night.
I sat at peace passing bobbipins
from a marshmallow pink cosmetic purse
embossed with jazzmen,
girls with pony tails and a November
10 topaz lucky birthstone.
They doused my cow's-lick, rollered
and skewered tightly.
I expected that to be lovely
would be worth the hurt.

15 They read my Stars,
tied chiffon scarves to doorhandles, tried
to teach me tight dancesteps
you'd no guarantee
any partner you might find would ever be able to
20 keep up with as far as I could see.

There were always things to burn
before the men came in.

For each disaster
you were meant to know the handy hint.
25 Soap at a pinch
but better nail varnish (clear) for ladders.
For kiss curls, spit.
Those days womanhood was quite a sticky thing
and that was what these grim sisters came to mean.

30 'You'll know all about it soon enough.'
But when the clock struck they
stood still, stopped dead.
And they were left there
out in the cold with the wrong skirtlength
35 and bouffant hair,
dressed to kill,
who'd been
all the rage in fifty-eight,
a swish of Persianelle
40 a slosh of perfume.
In those big black mantrap handbags
they snapped shut at any hint of that
were hedgehog hairbrushes
cottonwool mice and barbed combs to tease.
45 Their heels spiked bubblegum, dead leaves.

Wasp waist and cone breast, I see them yet.
I hope, I hope
there's been a change of more than silhouette.

Liz Lochhead

♦   The tone is established from the very beginning of the poem.

> And for special things
> (weddings, school-
> concerts) the grown up girls next door
> would do my hair.

The first word 'And' makes it sound as if we are breaking into the middle of a casual conversation. The words in brackets '(weddings, school-concerts)' continues this idea of details being casually added to a conversation.

♦   The next few lines have many unusual details of a teenage girl's world in the 1950s — Radio Luxembourg, bobbipins and pink cosmetic purse.

> 5   Luxembourg announced Amami Night.
>   I sat at peace passing bobbipins
>   from a marshmallow pink cosmetic purse
>   embossed with jazzmen,
>   girls with pony tails and a November
> 10   topaz lucky birthstone.
>   They doused my cow's-lick, rollered
>   and skewered tightly.
>   I expected that to be lovely
>   would be worth the hurt.

By adding 'marshmallow', the comic tone is conveyed. The purse sounds soft and squishy. The words 'doused' and 'skewered tightly' also suggests the comic tone. What do you imagine? A tight little sausage roller stabbed with a sharp spike? Even the final two lines are a humorous comment on teenage appearances — 'I expected that to be lovely / would be worth the hurt.'

♦   The next six lines are almost mocking in creating a complex but artificial world.

> 15   They read my Stars,
>   tied chiffon scarves to doorhandles, tried
>   to teach me tight dancesteps
>   you'd no guarantee
>   any partner you might find would ever be able to
> 20   keep up with as far as I could see.

These girls next-door read horoscopes, had 'chiffon' scarves (light and insubstantial) and they danced in ways that no partner could ever match because of the intricacy of the steps. The speaker is gently mocking the style of the grim sisters that she was studying and even imitating.

◆ Lines 21–22 are a bit puzzling and seem funny.

> There were always things to burn
> before the men came in.

What sort of 'things' do you imagine? Who would the men be?

◆ In lines 23–29, the details continue the mocking idea.

> For each disaster
> you were meant to know the handy hint.
> 25 Soap at a pinch
> but better nail varnish (clear) for ladders.
> For kiss curls, spit.
> Those days womanhood was quite a sticky thing
> And that was what these grim sisters came to mean.

This seems to be a list of handy hints for womanhood, such as nail varnish to stop ladders in tights — with 'clear' added in brackets to make it sound even more like important advice. The sisters would spit on curls and the speaker comments on womanhood being a 'sticky thing' using a slang phrase to mock this style of life.

◆ Can you detect a change of tone in lines 30–36?

> 30 'You'll know all about it soon enough.'
> But when the clock struck they
> stood still, stopped dead.
> And they were left there
> out in the cold with the wrong skirtlength
> 35 and bouffant hair,
> dressed to kill . . .

What words mark the change of tone? The phrase 'clock struck ' stands out and so does 'they / stood still, stopped dead'. The words in these lines are negative. The literal meaning of 'struck' sounds painful. Also 'dead', 'cold', 'wrong' and 'kill' are all negative words. 'Dressed to kill' is also a slang phrase, but if you take it literally it has an unpleasant suggestion. Is the poet trying to suggest in this stanza that there is something wrong with the way the sisters lived?

♦ Can you pick out any of the clichés or slang words that the poet uses in lines 37–45? (A cliché is an overused or trite expression — one that you have heard so often that it has lost its meaning.)

>   who'd been
>   all the rage in fifty-eight,
>   a swish of Persianelle
> 40 a slosh of perfume.
>   In those big black mantrap handbags
>   they snapped shut at any hint of that
>   were hedgehog hairbrushes
>   cottonwool mice and barbed combs to tease.
> 45 Their heels spiked bubblegum, dead leaves.

The speaker uses a number of clichés and slang words to suggest her criticism in these lines. Some of these phrases like 'all the rage' are typical of the slang of the 1950's. Also 'swish' and 'slosh'. The details in these lines, although they seem harmless enough, are actually described with painful words. Handbags are like 'big black mantraps' and they 'snap shut'. The image of hairbrushes like 'hedgehogs' also suggests spiky pain. 'Barbed' combs are used 'to tease' hair. The heels of shoes 'spiked' bubblegum. 'Dead leaves' has an ominous sound.

♦ The last lines of the poem confirm the speaker's (and the poet's) tone with more words and images of pain and sharpness.

>   Wasp waist and cone breast, I see them yet.
>   I hope, I hope
>   there's been a change of more than silhouette.

Women are shaped like wasps — small in the middle. And wasps sting. The final 'hope' is for a change. The poet is very critical of the artificial, one-dimensional, black and white world (silhouette) of the 1950s when she suggests that appearance was of utmost importance, that women were objects to be admired by men. The poet's attitude towards such superficiality and falseness is conveyed through words, images, punctuation, slang and cliché.

The poet's tone or attitude in this poem is fairly evident. It is a poem which should stimulate you to form opinions on the subject. Do you agree or disagree with the poet? Do you think that such attitudes towards women have been left in the past (in the 1950s) or are they still in evidence today?

And what about the title? Does it suggest anything to you — perhaps a fairy tale? Are there any words or ideas in the poem that you could use to support that suggestion?

Questions on *The Grimm Sisters*

Marks

1. What do the first four lines tell you about the speaker and the situation of the poem?

   2

2. *(a)* What details are there in lines 5–10 to support your ideas about the speaker and the situation in the first stanza? You should comment on two.

   4

   (b) How does the speaker of the poem accept the attention she is being given?
   Comment on two words or phrases in lines 5–14.

   4

3. In lines 15–22, there are details which suggest more about this teenage world. Choose two of the following and suggest what it tells you about the girls' activities:

   'my Stars' (line 15);
   'tied chiffon scarves to door handles' (line 16);
   'tight dance steps' (line 17);
   'things to burn' (line 21).

   4

4. How would you describe the tone of poem which is beginning to become more apparent in stanza 5 (lines 23–29)? Quote two of the words or phrases in these lines and show how it suggests this tone to you.

   4

5. (a) Explain how the word 'But' marks a turning point in the poem.

   2

   (b) Go on to comment on two colloquial words or phrases which suggest all is not well in lines 31–40.

   2

6. There are four unusual descriptions at the end of stanza six (lines 41–45). Comment on two of them, explaining how they can be seen as being negative or disagreeable or even frightening:

   'big black mantrap handbags . . . snapped shut' (lines 41–42);
   'hedgehog hairbrushes' (line 43);
   'barbed combs to tease' (line 44);
   'Their heels spiked bubblegum' (line 45).

   4

7. Say in your own words what the poet hopes for in lines 46–48.

   2

8. What does the title mean now that you understand the poem better?

   2

   Total marks   (30)

Questions on *The Grimm Sisters* with answer advice.

1. **What do the first four lines tell you about the speaker and the situation of the poem?**

    2

    First questions are meant to help you define the speaker or persona in the poem and the situation. They may ask what is happening. You should not answer in too much detail at this stage.

    What clues are there in this stanza about the speaker? 'grown-up girls next door'. This makes it sound as if the speaker is a girl or a woman and she seems to be recalling incidents in the past. She might be reflecting on when she was a child.

    Is there anything else you notice that is unusual and perhaps relevant to the situation? You might add that the poem starts with the word 'And' as if we — as readers or listeners — are breaking into the middle of a conversation.

    So your answer might be:

    The speaker of the poem seems to be a girl or a woman. She seems to be remembering events in her childhood when the older girls next door helped her to fix her hair for a special occasion.

2. *(a)* **What details are there in lines 5–10 to support your ideas about the speaker and the situation in the first stanza? You should comment on two.**

    4

    The details in these lines seem particularly feminine — and possibly also a bit old-fashioned — the 1950s or 1960s.

    You might comment on 'bobbipins' which few girls use any more in their hair or you might comment on the description of the purse — 'marshmallow pink cosmetic purse embossed with jazzman'. You can almost picture it — as a sort of teenage object of the past. 'Girls with pony tails' is also a feminine and youthful detail. Many girls when they are young also have a piece of jewellery with their birthstone which they consider lucky,

    You may or may not know that Radio Luxembourg was a popular station for teenagers in the 1950s, but there are enough other details to choose that you would not have to know that.

    For four marks you would select two details and try to make a fairly detailed comment on each. For example:

    The cosmetic purse is an obviously feminine item and also seems like something a young teenager might have since it has jazzmen printed on it. The colour pink makes it very girlish and the word 'marshmallow' just reinforces the colour and the texture.

Marks

2. *(b)* **How does the speaker of the poem accept the attention she is being given?**
   Comment on two words or phrases in lines 5–14.   **4**

   It is fairly obvious that there are two places to focus for this answer, both using the word 'I'. For four marks, you want to find these two places and make a comment on each of them.

   In line 6, it says 'I sat at peace'. You can imagine her sitting quietly while the girls are curling and fussing about her hair. In fact, she even passes them the bobbipins.

   In line 13, it says, 'I expected that to be lovely would be worth the hurt.' You can imagine that occasionally the girls would poke her too hard with a bobbipin or pull her hair too tightly when they rollered it, but she would accept passively the little pain.

3. **In lines 15–22, there are details which suggest more about this teenage world. Choose two of the following and suggest what it tells you about the girls' activities**

   > **'my Stars' (line 15);**
   > **'tied chiffon scarves to door handles' (line 16);**
   > **'tight dance steps' (line 17);**
   > **'things to burn' (line 21).**   **4**

   You should choose any two that you feel you can comment on most fully. Use your imagination in your comments. Do not just state the obvious but give connotations or suggestions that arise from the details. For example:

   'Stars' refers to horoscopes. It could suggest the idea of looking to the future or of fortune-telling. Horoscopes are not reality.

   'Chiffon' is a soft, flimsy material. It could suggest the artificiality of this teenage world, or the superficiality of their dress. It also suggests a style that was temporary, that would pass away with time.

   The 'tight dance steps' also suggest something that was popular at the time, a passing craze. It suggests that the girls knew the steps, but the boys probably did not know them very well. The dances are almost like routines, particular to this little set in society at that particular time.

   'Things to burn' also suggest that the girls had secrets from the men — perhaps notes or pictures or mementos. These would be items that would keep the girls separate from the men.

4. **How would you describe the tone of poem which is beginning to become more apparent in stanza 5 (lines 23–29)? Quote two of the words or phrases in these lines and show how it suggests this tone to you.**   **2**

Tone — the attitude of the poet or the speaker of the poem towards the subject. Some tones are fairly easy to recognise — such as humour. Or sarcasm: you are very clever, aren't you? — when the speaker is really meaning the opposite.

Sometimes words which reveal tone stand out a bit, are somewhat different from the rest of the context.

This particular stanza seems humorous, or tongue-in-cheek, as if the woman looking back on her girlhood is now poking fun at some of the things that she did then. You could even say that her tone seems a bit critical. There is a lot you could say about the tone that is beginning to emerge. Pupils often think that questions about tone are very difficult. Try to hear the poet's voice in the same way that you would listen for the tone in a speaker's voice. Is the poet being sarcastic?

What tells me that she might be sarcastic? You might get a mark for naming an appropriate tone, but what is much more important is your comment on some aspect of the language — the word choice, the sentence structure, the punctuation, the exaggeration, the details that tell you what the tone is. In other words, your proof is what is important in the answer. For example:
The word 'disaster' is a bit strong for the type of events being discussed — a ladder in tights or a fallen curl. The poet might be being sarcastic.

The phrase 'handy hint' also sounds as if she might be mocking some of the tricks they had — a bit like the title in a girls' magazine perhaps — 'Handy Hints for Housewives'.

Her language is all very colloquial which suggests that she might be treating her subject humorously — 'at a pinch' — meaning if you do not have what you need in an emergency.

Also 'ladders', 'kiss curls', 'spit' and 'sticky things' are colloquial and lighthearted.

The punctuation also contributes to the tone. The lack of sentences makes her tone sound offhand, casual or humorous. And the word 'clear', in parenthesis is a funny detail — almost for the simple-minded.

5 **(a) Explain how the word 'But' marks a turning point in the poem.**   **2**

The word 'but' is often a turning point or sometimes it is 'however'. These words suggest that the poet is about to give you another point of view. You should be able to describe what the picture, scene, idea or situation is like before the word 'but' and then describe what it is like after the word. This question is asking you how the mood or atmosphere changes. You might answer:

The mood in these stanzas before the word 'But' was cheerful and light-hearted, describing a teenage girl's world that seemed happy, if somewhat artificial and superficial.

After the word 'But', the scene seems darker or ominous. The 'clock struck' and all the cheerful activity stopped.

Marks

5. (b) **Go on to comment on two colloquial words or phrases which suggest all is not well in lines 31– 40.** 2

You might choose any of the words with negative suggestions or connotations:

'clock struck' might remind you of the fairy tale story of Cinderella;

'stood still' suggests that all the cheerful activity stopped.

The word 'dead' always has a frightening sound, even when it is used to mean stopped on the spot.

The word 'cold' is also used in a colloquial way here. It does not literally mean that the girls were locked out of the house in the snow, but that they were left out — not included.

The word 'wrong' also has negative suggestions that they were no longer doing things right.

The word 'kill' has negative suggestions of destruction although it is also used here in a colloquial or slang way here.

Also 'all the rage' is also a colloquial phrase, but literally it sounds very threatening for rage is extreme anger.

6. **There are four unusual descriptions at the end of stanza six (lines 41– 45). Comment on two of them explaining how they can be seen as being negative or disagreeable or even frightening:**

  'big black mantrap handbags . . . snapped shut' (lines 41– 42);
  'hedgehog hairbrushes' (line 43);
  'barbed combs to tease' (line 44);
  'Their heels spiked bubblegum' (line 45). 4

These descriptions are all consistent in seeming dangerous and even deadly. You need to ask yourself now why the poet is using such descriptions.

You can imagine the large handbags that are being described. Making them 'black' and calling them 'mantraps' suggests in a funny way their dangerous quality.

The bristles of a hedgehog are spiky and painful so this description also sounds frightening.

The word 'barbed' means spiky and sharp like barbed wire so a barbed comb has suggestions of pain along with the word 'tease' which might suggest knotted hair.

The heels of the shoes are 'spiked' and that word means sharp, pointed and potentially dangerous.

7. **Say in your own words what the poet hopes for in the last stanza (lines 46–48).**

You should, by this stage in your understanding of the poem, be able to appreciate certain details. You could answer:

The speaker seems to be hoping that women have changed in more ways than just appearance since these days when they were sharp, pointed, setting traps for catching men.

The phrase 'wasp waist' means very small and neat in the centre like a wasp, but also wasps sting and cause pain.

The phrase 'cone breast' sounds sharp and pointed and artificial.

The word 'silhouette' means black, usually flat, one-dimensional. It could mean that the poet is criticising harshly these grim sisters for having no real feelings or depth of personality. They are not real or genuine — just artificial representations.

8. **What does the title mean to you now that you understand the poem better?**

As long as you can firmly support your ideas by drawing upon words and details from the poem as proof, that is good. In fact, it might open some interesting discussion on varying interpretations of the poem. Some comments might be:

The word 'grim' suggests that now the speaker in the poem realises more fully what these neighbour girls were like. In the beginning she might have sat peacefully in childish innocence and let them curl her hair. As she grew up (and as the poem progressed), she became more critical of their tricks and ways.

She now has a different idea of what it means to be a woman and it is not so much a secret society or 'sisterhood' as these representations of a bygone era might have suggested. The title also suggests perhaps (along with 'the clock struck'), the idea of Cinderella and her evil sisters.

The poem seems to be presenting in a fairly light-hearted way — but yet critical — some comments on the artificiality and superficiality of femininity in the past.

TEXTUAL ANALYSIS

FOOTBALL AT SLACK

metaphor suggesting horse-back
or a small boat

Between (plunging) valleys, on a (bareback) of hill

Men in (blunting) colours   What are 'blunting' colours?

Bounced, and their blown ball bounced.   — alliteration of 'b' sound emphasises movement

ball 'jumped' like men jump

The blown ball jumped, and the merry-coloured men

5   Spouted (like water) to head it.   simile — men are like water in flowing movements

The ball blew away downwind —

continued repetition of 'b' — like continued movement of ball

men sound like rubber balls — bounce?

The (rubbery men) bounced after it.

ball sounds like men again — 'jumped'

The (ball jumped up) and out and hung on the wind

Over a gulf of treetops.

10   Then they all shouted together, and the ball blew back.   — alliteration

First three stanzas have many verbs — for constant motion

metaphor — sun peeking through opening in the clouds

Winds from (fiery holes in heaven)

(Piled the hills) darkening around them   stormy sky

To awe them. The glare light

(Mixed its mad oils) and threw glooms.   like an oil painting — light in sky

15   Then the rain lowered a steel press.   — metaphor — sounds like rain coming down heavily in spikes

very wet   walking in water

(Hair plastered), they all just trod water

more water   (To puddle glitter). And their shouts bobbed up   like drowning or swimming   } very wet stanza

Coming fine and thin, washed and happy

the hills   sounds like swimming

While the (humped world) (sank foundering)

20   And the valleys (blued unthinkable)   colour of the sky — like ink

Under the depth of Atlantic depression —

strong verbs — constant motion

But the wingers leapt, they bicycled in air

And the goalie flew horizontal   — suggests his movement — parallel to the ground

And once again a (golden holocaust)   metaphor for the sun — holocaust is a fire

25   (Lifted the cloud's edge), to watch them.   Personification — like sun lifting blanket of clouds

viewpoint — looking down on game from above — sees the whole scene

Ted Hughes

UNDER THE MOUNTAIN How can you be under the mountain?

Seen from above — looking down from the sky

sounds soft

The (foam) in the curving bay is a goose-quill — metaphor — edge of sea with white waves like feather

That feathers . . . unfeathers . . . itself. — suggests movement of water in and out

still looking down

Seen from above

From above haycocks look flat

5 The field is a flap and the haycocks buttons — metaphor — field is like a patch of cloth or pocket — buttoned

To keep it flush with the earth

repetition

Seen from above

house looks quiet

The house is a (silent) gadget whose purpose

Was a long since (obsolete). — means out-of-date — no longer used

Suggests a change

new perspective — 'you' and 'down'

10 (But) when (you) get down

The breakers are cold scum and the wrack — the sea close-up is scummy and cold

sound of sea on shore

unpleasant smell

(Sizzles) with (stinking) life.

negative

When (you get down) — repetition of perspective

The field is a (failed) or a worth-while crop, the source

15 Of back-ache if not (heartache). — feelings — negative — pain — disappointment

hard work — negative

And when you get down — repetition

emotions

The house is a (maelstrom*) of (loves and hates) where (you) —

storm or turmoil

(Having got down) — (belong). Final word of poem — emphasises being part of — belonging in emotional sense

Parenthetical expression — emphasising position 'down'

Louis MacNeice

THE FIFTH SENSE {
see
hear
taste
touch
smell
}

Lamps burn all the night —nurses watching patients

hospital or Infirmary (Here), where people must be watched and (seen),— sight — patients must be watched

And (I), a shepherd, Nicolis Loizou, — name of speaker
first person   Old shepherd in hospital

Wish for the (dark), for I have been — Could he be wishing for death?

5   Sure-footed in the dark, but now my sight —How can sight stumble

Stumbles among these (beds), (scattered white boulders), — metaphor — beds like rocks on hillside

As I lean towards my far slumbering house — his last resting place — death?

With the (night) lying upon my shoulders. — like a burden he is carrying

change to past tense

My (sight) (was) always good, — sight = first sense — was good

— taste — second sense
10   Better than others, I could (taste) wine and bread exceptional — could distinguish neighbours' wines and breads

And name the field they spattered when the harvest

enjambment

Broke. I could (coil) in the (red) — smell — could smell the fox
                            How can a scent have a colour?
(Scent) of the fox out of a maze of wood mixture of senses

And grass. I could (touch) mist, I could (touch) breath. touch — how can you touch mist and breath? almost invisible

15   But of my sharp senses I had only (four). only four senses

The (fifth) one (pinned) me to my death.
              must be hearing   'pinned' — negative — like pinning something down
    The Fifth Sense

The soldiers must have called — thinks they called but does not know

The word they needed: Halt. Not hearing it, — deaf — could not hear command

metaphor —I was their failure, relaxed against the (winter) — suggests end of life
                                    cold — 'dead of winter'
20   Sky, the flag of their defeat. shepherd hung like a limp flag in the sky
                        failed to move on soldiers' command

With their five senses they could not have told — they could not recognise the difference in him
hearing

That I lacked (one), and so they had to shoot.
                               obligation of soldiers to kill the disobedient

They would fire at a rainbow if it had

A colour less than they were taught. — rainbow — a natural phenomenon
    soldiers could not appreciate difference
    soldiers must have everything the same

25   Christ said that when one sheep   Christ's biblical teaching
of lost sheep

Was lost, the rest meant nothing any more.

return to the present

(Here in this hospital), where others' breathing — regularity of breathing

Swings (like a lantern) in the polished floor — breathing 'swings' like a pendulum

simile   — breathing = sound, lantern = sight

And squeezes those who cannot sleep,   *mixture of senses*

30   I see how precious each thing is, how (dear),

For I may never touch, smell, taste or see — final rhyme emphasises last word
     ①   ②   ③   ④

Again, because I could not (hear). — last word 'hear' — 'The Fifth Sense'

last two lines are rhythmic — monosyllables
         reminds us of title

Patricia Beer

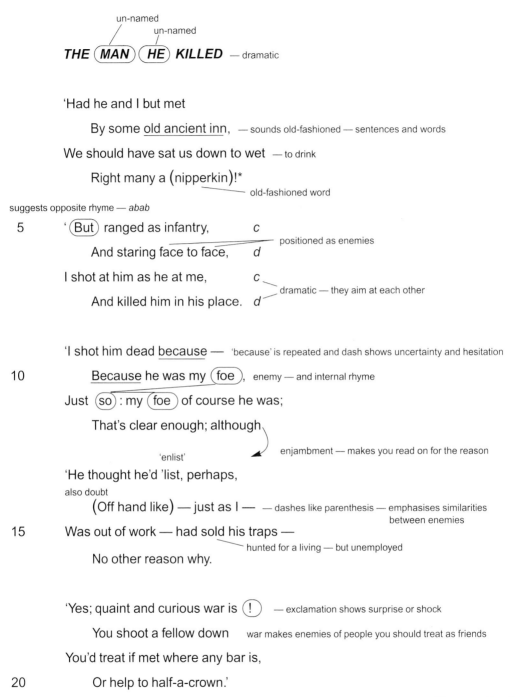

un-named

un-named

THE (MAN) (HE) KILLED — dramatic

'Had he and I but met

By some <u>old ancient inn</u>, — sounds old-fashioned — sentences and words

We should have sat us down to wet — to drink

Right many a (nipperkin)!*

old-fashioned word

suggests opposite rhyme — *abab*

5 ' (But) ranged as infantry, c

positioned as enemies

And staring face to face, d

I shot at him as he at me, c

dramatic — they aim at each other

And killed him in his place. d

'I shot him dead <u>because</u> — 'because' is repeated and dash shows uncertainty and hesitation

10 <u>Because</u> he was my (foe), enemy — and internal rhyme

Just (so) : my (foe) of course he was;

That's clear enough; although

'enlist'

enjambment — makes you read on for the reason

'He thought he'd 'list, perhaps,

also doubt

(Off hand like) — just as I — — dashes like parenthesis — emphasises similarities between enemies

15 Was out of work — had sold his traps —

hunted for a living — but unemployed

No other reason why.

'Yes; quaint and curious war is (!) — exclamation shows surprise or shock

You shoot a fellow down war makes enemies of people you should treat as friends

You'd treat if met where any bar is,

20 Or help to half-a-crown.'

Thomas Hardy

IN MRS TILSCHER'S CLASS — in school

You could travel up the Blue Nile — geography class

with your finger, tracing the route

while Mrs Tilscher (chanted) the scenery. — suggests repetition — even boredom

Tana. Ethiopia. Khartoum. Aswan. — exotic places

5   That for an hour, then a (skittle) of milk — strange word

and the (chalky) Pyramids rubbed into dust. — two meanings — blackboards and pyramids

A window opened with a long pole. — details of school

The (laugh of a bell) swung by a running child. — suggests happiness and freedom
personification — sounds happy

This was better than home. (Enthralling) books. — positive word — enjoyable

10   The classroom glowed (like a sweetshop). simile — class is attractive

Sugar paper. Coloured shapes. Brady and Hindley — odd — the child murderers

faded, (like the faint, uneasy smudge of a mistake). — simile — they are like a grey smudge

Mrs Tilscher (loved) you. Some mornings, you found — positive

she'd left a good (gold star) by your name. more school details — positive

15   The (scent of a pencil) slowly, carefully, shaved. ⎰ senses —
                                                      ⎱ smell — pencil shavings
A (xylophone's nonsense) heard from another form. sound — xylophone playing

Over the Easter term, the (inky) tadpoles changed — suggests dark colour of tadpoles like a blob of ink

change
of   from (commas into exclamation) marks. Three frogs — suggests shape
time
hopped in the playground, freed by a dunce,

20   followed by a line of kids, jumping and croaking — verbs = action on playground

away from the lunch queue. (A rough boy) — facts of life — the bad boy

told you how you were born. You kicked him, but stared
the facts of life
at your parents, (appalled), when you got back home. — negative word — emotional
                                                       — horror at hearing what
                                                         rough boy said

63

hot, sultry

alive — charged

That (feverish July), the air (tasted of electricity).

you can feel it

25 A (tangible) alarm made you always untidy, hot,

pathetic fallacy — weather like
the girl — changing — volatile

irritable

(fractious) under the heavy, sexy sky. You asked her

lack of response

how you were born and Mrs Tilscher smiled,

then turned away. Reports were handed out.

entry to freedom

You ran (through the gates), impatient to be grown,

30 as the sky (split open) into a thunderstorm. — thunderstorm = metaphor?

sounds violent, even painful

realisation of facts of life

Contrast between what is taught in class and what is learned in playground
Classroom is safe and happy and colourful
Playground and 'July' seems rough and images are negative
Tadpoles are symbolic of change

Carol Ann Duffy

CHILDHOOD

long broad vowels — sound long   'sunny' = pleasant

Long time he lay upon the sunny hill,   *a*

    To his father's house below securely bound.   *b*

        safety, security

Far off the silent, changing sound was still, — quiet   *a*

   negative

    With the (black) islands lying thick around.   *b*

            separate shapes in foreground — more vague in distance

5   He saw each separate height, each vaguer hue,   *c*

    Where the massed islands rolled in mist away,   *d*

   And though all ran together in his view — one view   *c*

metaphor — suggests dangers

    He knew that (unseen straits) between them lay.   *d*

            new experiences

   Often he wondered (what new shores) were there.   *e*

10   In thought he saw the still light on the sand,   *f*

         positive words — peace and happiness

   The shallow water clear in tranquil air,   *e*   suggest long walk

    And walked through it in (joy) from (strand) to (strand). *f*

   Over the sound a ship so slow would pass   long, broad, slow   *g*

                     vowel sounds

    That in the black hill's (gloom) it seemed to lie.   *h*

           negative word

                    simile — sea is like glass

15   The evening sound was smooth (like sunken glass),   *g*

    And time seemed finished ere the ship passed by.   *h*

              time drags

could be dangers lurking

    (Grey tiny rocks) slept round him where he lay,   *i*

                 passage of time

    Moveless as they, more still as (evening) came,   *j*   evening = darkness

                          could be negative

   The grasses threw straight (shadows) far away,   *i*

20   And from the house his mother called his name.   *j*

       reminder of security of beginning

Edwin Muir

LATE

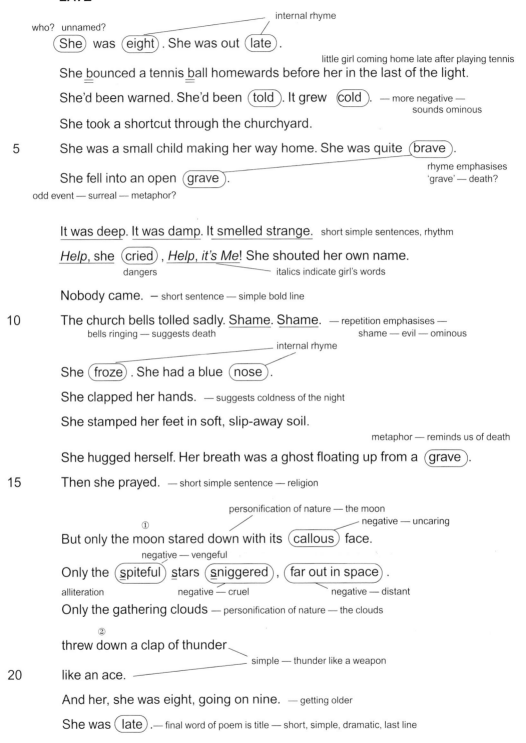

who? unnamed?

internal rhyme

(She) was (eight) . She was out (late) .

little girl coming home late after playing tennis

She bounced a tennis ball homewards before her in the last of the light.

She'd been warned. She'd been (told). It grew (cold). — more negative — sounds ominous

She took a shortcut through the churchyard.

5   She was a small child making her way home. She was quite (brave).

rhyme emphasises 'grave' — death?

She fell into an open (grave).

odd event — surreal — metaphor?

It was deep. It was damp. It smelled strange.   short simple sentences, rhythm

Help, she (cried) , *Help, it's Me*! She shouted her own name.

dangers   italics indicate girl's words

Nobody came.   — short sentence — simple bold line

10   The church bells tolled sadly. Shame. Shame.   — repetition emphasises —

bells ringing — suggests death   shame — evil — ominous

internal rhyme

She (froze) . She had a blue (nose).

She clapped her hands.   — suggests coldness of the night

She stamped her feet in soft, slip-away soil.

metaphor — reminds us of death

She hugged herself. Her breath was a ghost floating up from a (grave).

15   Then she prayed.   — short simple sentence — religion

personification of nature — the moon

①   negative — uncaring

But only the moon stared down with its (callous) face.

negative — vengeful

Only the (spiteful) stars (sniggered) , (far out in space) .

alliteration   negative — cruel   negative — distant

Only the gathering clouds — personification of nature — the clouds

②
threw down a clap of thunder

simple — thunder like a weapon

20   like an ace.

And her, she was eight, going on nine. — getting older

She was (late).— final word of poem is title — short, simple, dramatic, last line

Carol Ann Duffy

66

powerful force

(**STORM**) **ON THE ISLAND** — island is isolated, lonely surrounded
by a powerful force — water

note 'we' not 'I' (lonely)

(**We**) are prepared (**:**) we build our houses squat, ①
colon introduces preparations for storm — ways of building house

Sink walls in rock and roof them with good slate.

② negative — infertile ③
This (**wizened**) earth has never troubled us — unproductive land, little grows

With hay, so, as you see, there are no s<u>t</u>acks

5 Or s<u>t</u>ooks that can be lost. (Nor are there trees) — treeless landscape suggests
barrenness, isolation

Which might prove company <u>when it blows full</u> — monosyllables emphasise force of storm

<u>Blast</u> (**:**) you know what I mean — leaves and branches
colon introduces further explanation

Can raise a tragic chorus in a gale — metaphor — storm sounds like a chorus
trees can sound mournful

change of pronoun to 'you'

So that (**you**) listen to the thing you fear
punches — like a fight

10 Forgetting that it (**pummels**) your house too.

reminder that there are no breaks in the landscape
(**But**) there are no trees, no natural shelter.

You might think that the sea is <u>company,</u> — repetition of 'company' — need for
companionship

oxymoron
(**Exploding comfortably**) down on the cliffs — sound of sea on rocks

(**But**) no: when it begins, (**the flung spray <u>hits</u>**) — sounds like throwing stones —
suggests danger / pain

15 The very windows, <u>spits</u> (**like a tame <u>cat</u>**) — simile — spray is like an angry cat
hissing and spitting

dangerous / wild
Turned (**savage**). We just s<u>i</u>t t<u>i</u>ght while wind vies — clipped 't' sounds
sea can change and be angry

And strafes invisibly. Space is a salvo,

suggests war
We are (**bombarded**) by the empty air.

oxymoron
(**Strange**), it is a (**huge nothing**) that we fear.

important   suggests greatness and nothingness —
first word of   wind is actually invisible or 'nothing'
last line

need for companionship —
feeling of isolation / loneliness / vulnerability

Seamus Heaney

RAIN

A motorbike breaks down near Sanna in (torrential) rain,

adjective describing rain is very dramatic

Pouring loud enough to perforate limousines, long enough

metaphor — makes rain sound like knives

exaggeration

(To wash us to Belize). Partick's

exaggeration — to emphasise amount of rain

(Fish-scaled) with wetness. Drips shower from foliage, cobbles, tourists

5   From New York and Dusseldorf at the tideline >   *list of the wetness*

Shoes lost in bogs, soaked in potholes, clarted with glaur.   *— Scottish words*

And old woman is splashed by a bus. A gash >

unusual line break — enjambment — metaphor describing heavy rain storm

In cloud. Indians

Arrived this week to join their families and who do not feel

10   Scottish one inch push onwards into a drizzle >   *drizzle turns to downpour*

That gets heavy and vertical. Golf umbrellas

simile — the colours are exotic, the sudden opening of orchids like opening of umbrellas

Come up like orchids on fast-forward film; exotic

describes the colour

(Cagoules fluoresce nowhere), speckling a hillside, and plump.

Off dykes and gutters, overflowing   *still lists all the evidence of wetness*

15   Ditches, a granary of water drenches the shoulders

Of Goatfell and Schiehallion. Maps under Perspex go bleary, >   *maps on display at famous sites*

Spectacles clog, Strathclyde, Tayside, Dundee >   *writing about whole of Scotland*

Catch it, fingers spilling with water, oil-stained

As it comes down in sheets, blows

short sentence draws attention to ceaseless rain

20   Where there are no trees, snow-set. [Without thought of the morrow.]

Weddings, prunes, abattoirs, strippers, Glen Nevis, snails

? what does this mean? — everything and everyone gets wet

(Blur in its democracy), down your back, on your breasts.

all Scottish places

In Kilmarnock a child walks naked. A woman laughs.

In cars, in Tiree bedrooms, in caravans and tenements,

?

25   Couples sleeved in love, the (gibbous) Govan rain.

Robert Crawford

STEALING

question — sounds like speaker repeating a question she has been asked

The most unusual thing I ever stole (?) A snowman.   single dramatic answer

another single word answer

(Midnight). He looked magnificent; a tall, white (mute) — silent

beneath the winter moon. I wanted him, a mate — alliteration — *m* sounds draws
attention to snowman

with a mind (as cold as the slice of ice) — simile — sound is interesting

5   within my own brain. I started with the head.

taking snowman apart — sounds painful

Better off dead than giving in, not taking

what you want. He weighed a ton, his torso,

frozen stiff, hugged to my chest, (a fierce chill — negative sound — seems painful

piercing my gut). Part of the thrill was knowing — likes pain — likes to hurt others

10   that children would cry in the morning. Life's tough.

Sometimes I steal things I don't need. I joy-ride cars
revealing — speaker tells
to nowhere, break into houses just to have a look.   about himself

I'm a mucky ghost, leave a mess, maybe pinch a camera. — colloquial language

I watch my gloved hand twisting the doorknob.

15   (A stranger's bedroom). (Mirrors). (I sigh like this). — *Aah*. — short sentences —
even incomplete

(It took some time). (Reassembled in the yard),

he didn't look the same. I took a run

dramatic repetition — draws attention to actions
and booted him. Again. Again. My breath ripped out — interesting phrase

in rage. It seems daft now. Then I was standing

20   alone amongst lumps of snow, sick of the world.

single word sentence draws attention

Boredom. Mostly I'm so bored I could eat myself.— exaggeration odd

One time, I stole a guitar and thought I might

learn to play. I nicked a bust of Shakespeare once,   steals strange items
— colloquial words

flogged it, but the snowman was strangest.

final sentence is a question —
25   You don't understand a word I'm saying, do you?   reminds us of question at beginning
is it an interview situation between two people?

Carol Ann Duffy

69

unusual word — why 'grim'?

THE (GRIMM) SISTERS

sounds like the middle of a discussion

And for special things

(weddings, school-   parenthesis — example of special occasions

concerts) the grown up girls next door

would do my hair.

5   Luxembourg announced Amami Night.   — radio of the 1970s

I sat at peace passing bobbipins

from a marshmallow pink cosmetic purse   > details of purse — dated

embossed with jazzmen,

girls with pony tails and a November

10   topaz lucky birthstone.   > trinkets of teenage years

They doused my cow's-lick, rollered

and skewered tightly.   — metaphor — makes hair sound like sausage

I expected that to be lovely

would be worth the hurt.   > humour shows Scottish naïveté

15   They read my Stars,   — horoscopes

tied chiffon scarves to doorhandles, tried

to teach me tight dancesteps   > things poet learned from teenage neighbours

you'd no guarantee

any partner you might find would ever be able to

20   keep up with as afar as I could see.   humour shown in childish perspective

There were always things to burn > what kind of things?

before the men came in.— what men? boyfriends?

70

For each disaster

you were meant to know the handy hint. beauty tips for teenagers

25 Soap at a pinch

but better nail varnish (clear) for ladders.
detail in parenthesis
For kiss curls, spit.

Those days womanhood was quite a sticky thing   humour — a 'sticky thing' makes
being a woman sound messy
and that was what these grim sisters came to mean.

30 'You'll know all about it soon enough.' — words of the sisters

But when the clock struck they
— like Cinderella
stood still, stopped dead.

And they were left there

out in the cold with the wrong skirtlength   all negative words — all goes wrong with sisters

35 and bouffant hair,

dressed to kill, — cliché — literal meaning is negative

who'd been

all the rage in fifty-eight,

a swish of Persianelle   more details of teenage girls growing up

40 a slosh of perfume.

In those big black mantrap handbags — negative words — to trap men

they snapped shut at any hint of that — personification

were hedgehog hairbrushes — hedgehogs are spiky and painful

cotton wool mice and barbed combs to tease. — all sharp words — potentially
wounding and painful
45 Their heels spiked bubblegum, dead leaves.

wasp's sting
Wasp waist and (cone) breast, I see them yet.
sharp and pointed
I hope, I hope
repetition emphasises wish
there's been a change of more than silhouette.
what does poet wish for? What changes does she want

Liz Lochhead

ACKNOWLEDGEMENTS

We hereby acknowledge the use of copyright material in this book
and are grateful to those for granting this permission.

Football at Slack from *River*
by Ted Hughes.
Reprinted by permission of the publisher Faber and Faber Ltd.

Under the Mountain from *Collected Poems*
by Louis MacNeice and published by Faber and Faber Ltd.
Reprinted by permission of David Higham Associates.

The Fifth Sense from *Collected Poems*
by Patricia Beer.
Reprinted by permission of the publisher Carcanet Press Ltd.

The Man He Killed
by Thomas Hardy (1840–1928).

In Mrs Tilscher's Class from *The Other Country*
by Carol Ann Duffy and published by Anvil Press Poetry Ltd., 1990.
Reprinted by permission of the publisher Anvil Press Poetry Ltd.

Childhood from *Collected Poems 1921–1958*
by Edwin Muir.
Reprinted by permission of the publisher Faber and Faber Ltd.

Late from *Meeting Midnight*
by Carol Ann Duffy.
Reprinted by permission of the publisher Faber and Faber Ltd.

Storm on the Island from *Death of a Naturalist*
by Seamus Heaney.
Reprinted by permission of the publisher Faber and Faber Ltd.

Rain from *A Scottish Assembly*
by Robert Crawford and published by Chatto & Windus.
Reprinted by permission of The Random House Group.

Stealing from *Selling Manhattan*
by Carol Ann Duffy published by Anvil Press Poetry in 1987.
Reprinted by permission of the publisher Anvil Press Poetry Ltd.

The Grimm Sisters
by Liz Lochhead
from *Dreaming Frankenstein and Collected Poems* Polygon 1984 (ISBN 0 7486 6158 1).
Reprinted by permission of the publisher Polygon.